King Confession:
PSALM 23

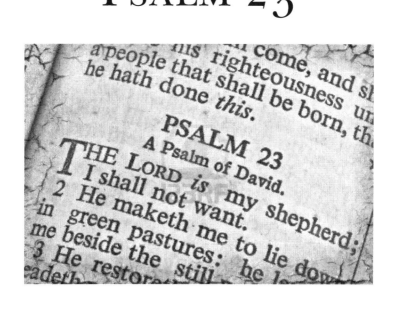

By H. Rondel Rumburg

SBSS
APPOMATTOX, VIRGINIA

SBSS

PO Box 472
SPOUT SPRING, VIRGINIA 24593

A LISTING OF OUR PUBLICATIONS AT

BiblicalAndSouthernStudies.com

The Second Coming of Christ, S. M. Merrill
The Gospel in Enoch, Henry H. Tucker

BOOKS BY H. RONDEL RUMBURG

Baptists and the State
Stonewall Jackson's Verse
William Bridge
John Pelham of Alabama
The Universal Dominion of Christ
The Songs of Southern Zion: Confederate Hymnology
The Soul Sufferings of Christ
"Stonewall" Jackson's Chaplain: Beverly Tucker Lacy
*"Stonewall" Jackson's Wife and Daughter: Mary Anna Jackson and
Julia Jackson Christian*
Ruth the Maiden from Moab
Cameos of Confederate Chaplains
Confederate Flags Matter: The Christian Influence on the Flags
"Charlie" and the Chaplain
Christmas in the Confederacy
A Christian Widows Handbook

THE LORD IS MY SHEPHERD: JEHOVAH-ROHI

PSALM 23
Authorized Version
A PSALM OF DAVID.

The LORD *is* my shepherd; I shall not want.

He maketh me to lie down in green pastures: he leadeth me beside the still waters.

He restoreth my soul: he leadeth me in the paths of righteousness for his name's sake.

Yea, though I walk through the valley of the shadow of death, I will fear no evil: for thou *art* with me; thy rod and thy staff they comfort me.

Thou preparest a table before me in the presence of mine enemies: thou anointest my head with oil; my cup runneth over.

Surely goodness and mercy shall follow me all the days of my life: and I will dwell in the house of the LORD for ever.

PSALM 23

From Miles Coverdale's Psalter
Dominus regit me

The Lord is my shepherd; therefore can I lack nothing.

He shall feed me in a green pasture, and lead me forth beside the waters of comfort.

He shall convert my soul, and bring me forth in the paths of righteousness, for his Name's sake.

Yea, though I walk through the valley of the shadow of death, I will fear no evil; for thou art with me; thy rod and thy staff comfort me.

Thou shalt prepare a table before me against them that trouble me; thou hast anointed my head with oil, and my cup shall be full. But thy loving-kindness and mercy shall follow me all the days of my life; and I will dwell in the house of the Lord for ever.

PSAL. XXIII.

Dauids confidence in Gods grace.

¶ A Pſalme of Dauid.

He LORD is * my ſhep-heard, I ſhall not want.

2 He maketh me to lie downe in † greene pa-ſtures: he leadeth mee be-ſide the † ſtill waters.

3 He reſtoreth my ſoule: he leadeth me in the pathes of righteouſnes, for his names ſake.

4 Yea though I walke through the valley of the ſhadowe of death,* I will feare no euill: for thou art with me, thy rod and thy ſtaffe, they comfort me.

5 Thou prepareſt a table before me, in the preſence of mine enemies : thou † anointeſt my head with oyle, my cuppe runneth ouer.

6 Surely goodnes and mercie ſhall followe me all the daies of my life : and I will dwell in the houſe of the LORD † for euer.

Psalm 23 from the 1611 first edition of the Authorized Version

PSALM 23
[Scottish Version, 1641]

The Lord's my Shepherd, I'll not want
He makes me down to lie
In pastures green: He leadeth me
The quiet waters by.

My soul He doth restore again,
And me to walk doth make
Within the paths of righteousness,
E'en for His own name's sake.

Yea, though I walk through death's dark vale,
Yet will I fear no ill:
For Thou art with me, and Thy rod
And staff me comfort still.

My table Thou hast furnished
In presence of my foes;
My head Thou dost with oil anoint,
And my cup overflows.

Goodness and mercy all my life
Shall surely follow me;
And in God's house for evermore
My dwelling place shall be.

Table of Contents

Foreword

The adage "familiarity breeds contempt" has been attributed to various persons including the Puritan Richard Baxter. It's message certainly finds an application with the Twenty-third Psalm. It is one of the best known and most recognizable of all Scriptures. It is recited on occasions of all kinds. It is often requested as a reading at funerals even from non-believers. The tendency would be to think of it then as being highly reverenced when in fact there may be few who hear it or read it that have anything other than a superficial understanding of it. They recognize to a degree poetic beauty, rhythm, and symmetry. They honor its traditional use in a ceremonial way. But, they neither know nor honor the Lord as their shepherd nor enter personally into the experience that David describes. Anything short of fully exalting this essential role of Christ in the life of believers is contempt.

Much has been written concerning the Psalm and it is worthy of such attention. It has been analyzed and exegeted from many perspectives and most may be read with great profit. The voluminous amount of material may lead one to ask, "What else can be said?" The perspective from which Dr. Rumburg approached his study in this Psalm is refreshing to say the least. He has plumbed the depths of the Psalm while maintaining a living objectivity regarding who wrote it and what is written. It is truly a confession of faith and one given under divine inspiration and we never lose sight of this as we proceed through the book. David is sharing his own experience with his reader and directing the attention of all to the Lord who is his Shepherd. The author of this book takes us by the hand and leads us to see who and what David saw and reinforces the experience with ample illustration and the call of many others to witness to the truths found herein. It is evident that such has been and is the experience of the author of this book.

An artist could depict the scenes the Psalmist describes and would no doubt be applauded at the pastoral rendering of it all. A witness could talk of having been there. When the Psalmist describes, in such high terms, his relationship with the Lord as his Shepherd, Dr. Rumburg bids us discover the same relationship in our own heart so that David's words become our words. When the Psalmist tells of the Lord making him "to lie down in green pastures," we are bidden to enter into such a repose as is directed by our Lord. And so, we are led through the Psalm with a view to both understanding of divine intent and experiencing what David enjoyed in the assurances he describes.

In each of these scenarios we are struck by the beauty of the figures used. But, we are further led to embrace each of them as our own. Each is made a matter of the heart as well as the mind. Each is made to fit beautifully in the composite picture of the identity of the Shepherd with His sheep. They hear His voice indeed and in following Him they blessedly and confidently discover what only the redeemed of the Lord may know – He is their Shepherd!

Many may be able to recite this Psalm by heart. Many may ably express the meaning of the various figures and even relate it to their own devotion to the Lord. We are taken, in this book, into the experience of David and the devotion of one who delights in sharing the treasures of the Lord with others. Many things already known and enjoyed are often made more sweet by being called to share them with another. The joys experienced by a dear brother will be to the delight of all who enter into these pages with the expectation of being renewed and refreshed in the wonders of The Lord our Shepherd. Even as we are led to what might be familiar territory we see the same things through another set of spiritual eyes and experience blessed confirmation and reconnection wherein Christ is exalted and we are built the more in the most holy faith.

It is certain that many saints have benefited greatly from reading the words of David and that many more shall. A re-visitation under the guidance of one skilled in presentation and personally touched by the experience is invaluable to all. That is what we have in this volume. I had previously heard Dr. Rumburg preach a good deal of what is found here. Even so, it was with wide-eyed and heavenly wonder that I gratefully digested these pages and so commend this work to all.

Brant H. Seacrist, Jr., Pastor
The Riverside Baptist Church
Richwood, WV

PSALM 23

[From *The Bay Psalm Book*,
the first book published in America, 1640]

The Lord to mee a sheapheard is,
 want therefore shall not I.
Hee in the folds of tender-grasse,
 doth cause mee downe to lie:

To waters calme me gently leads
 Restore my soule doth hee:
he doth in paths of righteousnes:
 for his names sake leade mee.

Yea though in valley of deaths shade
 I walk, none ill I'le feare:
because thou art with mee, thy rod,
 and staffe my comfort are.

For mee a table thou hast spread,
 in presence of my foes:
thou dost annoynt my head with oyle,
 my cup it over-flowes.

Goodnes and mercy surely shall
 all my days follow mee:
and in the Lords house I shall dwell
 so long as dayes shall bee.

Preface

During over fifty years in the pastorate the Psalms have been a spiritual boon in my own life and that of the congregations which I have been blessed to pastor. These sacred compositions have ministered, convicted, and encouraged my own heart. Some of my earliest memories as a boy were a result of the *Child's Bible Reader* that my mother read to us. I remember looking through this book at pictures, especially pictures of David as a lad holding a sling, as a giant slayer, and others. I do not know what became of that book, but a few years ago I was pleased to find a used copy. I believe it was the same 1949 edition Mom had. David, as a heroic person and as a child of God, loomed large in my mind and heart. He was the one used of God to write so many inspired hymns found in Scripture. He has had some part in my life since a child. I remember making a sling and trying to learn to use it. Alas, no accuracy was ever achieved although I thought I was one of Ehud's band of lefties.

The *Book of Psalms* is so filled with spiritual food for the hungry child of God; so filled with instruction for the teachable child of God; so filled with portraits of the glorious God of heaven and earth; so filled with the balm in Gilead to the healing of spiritual hurt; so filled with Christ my Saviour in the Messianic Psalms; so filled with the true expressions of the worship of my eternal God; so filled with comfort for the sorrowing child of God and my description could go on and on.

There have been certain Psalms that met a special need at a precise time in my life. One of those Psalms is Psalm 23. I believe this is the first one I memorized. I have often run beside the still waters only to stop and quench my spiritual thirst! Many are the times I have lain down in those restoring green pastures. I trust by the good grace of God to have Him walk with me through the valley of the shadow of death without fear and comforted by His rod and staff. Then to top it all off that I may dwell in His house forever.

As always I want to thank my dear wife Barbara for her care of me so that I might seek to express myself with words. Also, Pastor Brant Seacrist, I greatly appreciate your godly friendship of many years for writing the Foreword. The best to you and Suzie as we continue following our good, great, and glorious Shepherd in this journey to "The House of the LORD."

H. Rondel Rumburg
The Briar Patch
2017

Introduction

Psalm 23 like all God's inspired Word is a holy conveyance of precious truth unto those who need it for spiritual sustenance and guidance. Those introducing Obadiah Sedgwick's *The Shepherd of Israel* appended,

> The Holy Scriptures are conduit-pipes to convey unto particular uses those most precious Truths which are in general comprised in them.... Two special breasts of Consolation the Lord affords to Believers, that they may by Faith suck sweetest comfort from them, that is to say, special Promises and special Providence both which are so advantageously drawn out, and held out to believers.

Certainly Psalm 23 fits this depiction for it has been a harbinger of comfort to the saints throughout the centuries.

Edward Irving, in many ways a brilliant but tragic figure, who died of tuberculosis on the Lord's Day, December 7, 1834 at age 42. On his deathbed someone thought they heard him speaking in an unknown tongue. But his minister father-in-law, Dr. John Martin, listened to his sounds and found that Edward was reciting Psalm 23 in Hebrew. He murmured over and over again in Hebrew *Y'hovah ro'eh. The Lord is my Shepherd* was uttered in Hebrew and when he came to the latter verses the dying voice swelled and the observer, Rev. Martin, took up and echoed the wonderful strain—*Though I walk through the valley of the shadow of death, I will fear no evil.* As the current of life grew feebler and feebler, a last debate seemed to rise in that soul which was now hidden with God. At last that self argument came to a sublime conclusion in a trust stronger than life or death. As the gloomy December Sunday sank into the night shadows, his last audible words on earth fell from his pale lips. The last thing that could made out was,—"If I die, I die unto the Lord, Amen." And so, at the wintry midnight hour, which ended his last Sabbath on earth, the last bonds of mortal trouble dropped away, and he entered into the rest of the Lord his Shepherd.

As one approaches this Psalm there should be an awareness of its great benefit to multitudes of people. One is bowed down with a sense of ineptness in realizing the glorious character of God contained therein. Yet it is such a well worn spot in most Bibles because the Lord's people have so often turned there in times of trouble. Therein solace is sought in times that try the soul. Could David have gone to any greater height of expression? "He has endeavored to express the blessedness of his condition, in having the Lord for his shepherd, but after all his efforts he is conscious of failure. His sonnet has not reached the height of the great argument, nor has his soul, though enlarged with gratitude, been able to compass the immeasurable gifts of grace," proclaimed C. H. Spurgeon in one of his *Metropolitan Tabernacle Pulpit* sermons.

Oh, consider the importance of knowing the Shepherd of Psalm 23! Many years ago there was a group of people gathered in a drawing room. A famous actor was asked to make a recitation. He asked what he should recite. After a moment an old minister of the Gospel of Christ asked for Psalm 23. A strange look came on the actor's face and he

16

paused for a moment and then said, "I will, on one condition—that after I have recited it, you, my friend will do the same." The old preacher acquiesced by saying, "I am not an elocutionist, but, if you wish it, I shall do so." The actor began quoting the Psalm. His voice was modulated and intonated perfectly. The audience was spellbound, and as he finished there was a great burst of applause. After it died away, the old preacher rose to begin the Psalm. His voice was aged and not remarkable; his tone was flawed, but when he finished there was not a dry eye in the room. The actor rose and his voice quivered as he said, "Ladies and gentlemen, I reached your eyes and ears, but he has reached your hearts. The difference is just this: I know the Psalm but he knows the Shepherd! Oh, that we would through these expositions come to know the Shepherd more personally.

Psalm 23 is a glorious illustration borrowed from a common sight in the agrarian world in which it first appeared; for shepherds and sheep were a normal part of that world. Sheep were a critical link in daily life for they provided a primary source of food, clothing and shelter. The pastoral scene in the first part of this psalm is beautiful. The mind's eye seems to open and rest upon white sheep, green pastures and still clear waters with a shepherd leading about his flock. Some of the sheep are grazing at the shepherd's feet on lush grass and some are resting in the verdant pasture. Then some are quaffing their thirst from the still refreshing waters. The shepherd with a watchful eye is surveying his flock. How wonderful that God selects the poet-shepherd and by inspiration portrays that scene in a way to reveal to us His care towards His sheep. These sheep were purchased with the greatest price ever paid—the Lamb of God; that price was the gift of His Son. The Shepherd's sheep safely abide in His omnipotent, omniscient and omnipresent care.

What an instructive symbol—the shepherd. As the shepherd is to his flock, so God is to His people; and such as the sheep are to their shepherd, so are the believers to their caring Lord. One of the most beautiful summations of this psalm declares:

> The Twenty-third Psalm commends itself to the heart of the believer by its own internal excellence. Natural in its structure, simple and perspicuous in its language, and elegant and attractive in its imagery, it breathes forth sentiments of confidence towards God, of gratitude and of joy. There is a depth of meaning in every sentence—a rich variety of experience in every verse—and a fullness of joy from its commencement to its conclusion, which comprehends all that is needed in life and in death, in time and throughout eternity. The memoirs of departed Christians amply testify to this fact. How often has the Twenty-third Psalm been cited by the dying believer as a most appropriate expression of his past experience, his present feelings, and his future hopes! To multitudes of the faithful, this Psalm has doubtless proved a rich source of consolation, in every age since it was composed by the sweet singer of Israel [John Stevenson, *The Lord Our Shepherd*].

David in this psalm breaks out into this beautiful hymn, "The LORD is my shepherd!" In the first four verses he set forth what Jehovah the Shepherd did for his safety and his happiness. Suddenly he turned to introduce another picture wherein he represents his Lord not just as a tender

Shepherd who feeds His flock in pastures green, but as the princely Host of Heaven entertaining His guests with the most generous hospitality while spreading a banquet. From the view of a flock with its Shepherd the writer guides us to a royal banquet. This could indicate that Psalm 23 was written at a transition period in David's life whereby he went from being a shepherd boy to that of a prince.

When did David write this psalm?

At first glance one might think it was when he was a shepherd, but that would not be borne out by the entire psalm. Can we know for certain when it was written? In David's youth as a shepherd boy he kept his family's flock. He experienced many hardships and trials as a lad doing a shepherds duty. Even his brothers did not appear to be very encouraging. Young David did not grow up with a silver spoon in his mouth nor did he commence life drinking from a golden goblet. He was away from home most of the time providing safety and finding food and water for sheep. Along with this he sought to protect the sheep as they constantly faced fierce critters trying to destroy them. But this youth in his solace from human contact had the blessing of coming to know his great God and experiencing His intervention in his life on numerous occasions. At this time he grew deeply in his personal relationship with the Lord. His heart was exercised toward the Lord and he began to master the harp, he began to compose hymns to the Lord, singing praises to Jehovah the God of his salvation. The psalms David wrote are filled with a sense of the person of God.

When the Lord sought out a new king after rejecting Saul He sent His servant Samuel to the house of Jesse to find the next king. There Samuel considered seven sons one by one as Jesse had them pass before him. The Lord's servant asked if these were all his boys, and Jesse said he had one more; this one was the youngest and he was keeping the sheep. So Samuel requested that the youngest son be fetched. Jehovah spoke to His servant regarding David, "Arise, anoint him: for this is he." Samuel then anointed David's head with oil in the midst of his family and the Holy Spirit came on David from that time onward. However, the Spirit of Jehovah departed from Saul who thereafter was troubled by an evil spirit. King Saul then required a cunning player of the harp to calm him when that spirit accosted him. David's reputation on the harp had brought attention from the court and he was summonsed to provide the solace of his harp.

After this musical interlude at court David returned "from Saul to feed his father's sheep." Then on one occasion he was instructed by his father to take food to three of his brothers in the army, and before carrying out his father's commission he left his sheep in the care of another. David's brother Eliab became angry with him because he showed up and left the sheep in the wilderness. His brother said, "I know thy pride, and the naughtiness of thine heart; for thou art come down that thou mightiest see the battle." David asked, "What have I now done? Is there not a cause?" David became intensely disturbed when he observed the heathen Goliath's challenge and mockery of the God of Israel. David told King Saul that he would go and fight that Philistine to save his countrymen from heart failure. Saul reminded David of his inability to fight such a man for he was just a youth. David recited how he had tended his father's sheep which led him to destroy a lion and a bear thus saving the sheep. The shepherd boy said that this uncircumcised

Philistine would be just like those animals he had killed, because Goliath has defied the armies of the living God. Eventually the king told David to go and Jehovah would be with him. The king's armor was tried on David but he refused to use it because it had not been proved. So the shepherd boy took his staff, chose five smooth stones from the brook and put them in his pouch. Then he took his sling in his hand as he approached the Philistine.

The giant saw the lad with a fair countenance approaching and this disgusted him. Goliath considered this a great dishonor for he faced essentially no threat at all. This led him to say, "Am I a dog?" The wicked Philistine cursed David by his false gods and implored, "Come to me, and I will give thy flesh unto the fowls of the air, and to the beasts of the field." But David had some appropriate words of his own; for he told the giant, you are coming with a sword, spear and shield, but "I come to thee in the name of the LORD of hosts, the God of the armies of Israel, whom thou hast defied. This day will the LORD deliver thee into my hand; and I will smite thee, and take thine head from thee; and I will give the carcasses of the host of the Philistines this day unto the fowls of the air, and the wild beasts of the earth; that all the earth may know that there is a God in Israel."

There stood the God defying Goliath with a coat of armor weighting around one hundred and sixty pounds which was likely heaver than David's body weight soaking wet. As the giant drew near to David he began to run toward him and as he did David withdrew a stone out of his bag and sank the stone into the forehead of Goliath with his trusty sling. The giant fell on his face dead. David ran and stood upon the body of the giant, took his sword and cut his head off with it. The Philistine army had observed this act by a mere boy which caused them to flee in a panic. The men of Israel now began to pursue the enemy. David brought Goliath's head to Jerusalem along with his armor and put it in his tent. After this great exploit of David, in the name of the LORD of hosts, King Saul made him an officer in his army. When David returned from the slaughter a group of women played and sang a song that had been composed for the moment, "Saul hath slain his thousands, and David his ten thousands." This exaggerated song made the king angry and from that time on he was suspicious and premeditated a way to kill David.

After this an evil spirit from God came over Saul and David again was summonsed to play his harp, but the king twice threw a javelin at David seeking to fasten him to the wall, but each time David avoided the attempt on his life. The king sent him away at the head of a thousand soldiers thinking he would be overwhelmed leading to his death. But Jehovah was with David. These events increased Saul's fear of him as all Israel and Judah loved David. Saul then offered David his eldest daughter Merab to wife if he would fight the Philistines hoping they would kill him. The Lord preserved David again and when the king's daughter was due to be given him Saul had given her to another. Michal, Saul's daughter loved David so he gave her to David for a wife providing David kill a hundred Philistines and bring evidence of it. Again he hoped for David's death. The king also believed Michal would be a snare to David. David brought evidence of two hundred dead Philistines. Saul gave him Michal. Saul now knew that Jehovah was with David and that his daughter loved him along with all Israel.

All of this led to Saul's chagrin and fear; so the biblical account said he "became David's enemy continually."

Another matter that drove the anger of Saul was his son Jonathan's friendship with David. Saul in anger against his own son said, "Thou son of the perverse rebellious woman, do not I know that thou hast chosen the son of Jesse to thine own confusion, and unto the confusion of thy mother's nakedness?" David and Jonathan had made a solemn covenant of friendship each pledging to protect the other. When Jonathan's father sought to kill his friend he warned David. His wife Michal helped her husband escape on one occasion. When he escaped and sought Samuel he explained all that Saul had done. So David went with Samuel to dwell in Naioth but eventually he had to flee to Ramah. But David continued to keep in contact with his friend Jonathan.

Saul was determined to destroy David! David had accumulated six hundred followers and went to the wilderness near Ziph, which was about three miles south of Hebron. He was betrayed by the men of Ziph and David moved on again. Saul temporarily had to halt his pursuit of David because of attacks from the Philistine army. During this lull David moved to Engedi. It was during this time that he had the opportunity to kill Saul but would not do so. Upon discovering that David could have killed him Saul went home embarrassed. Then the man of God, David's friend and adviser, Samuel died.

David still on the run went to the wilderness of Paran. There he protected the flocks of Nabal from marauders. But Nabal mistreated David who planned an attack on Nabal, but Abigail, Nabal's wife, persuaded David to not do so. She took charge of seeing that they were supplied with food. After Nabal's death David married Abigail.

Again King Saul could not contain himself and pursued David in the wilderness of Ziph. When David spared his life again while the king slept, Saul temporarily stopped his pursuit. David did not think he could trust Saul so he became an ally with Achish king of Gath. Achish gave David and his men the town of Ziklag as a place to live. Here David remained for some sixteen months, the most stable domain he had known for a long time. Here was the base from which he and his men made their attacks.

At the Battle of Mount Gilboa Saul and his army were headed for defeat. When Saul realized he would be captured he fell on his sword. Saul died and so did three of his sons. An Amalekite who observed this sought to gain a reward by telling David that he had killed Saul. When David heard of the death of Jonathan and Saul he killed the Amalekite who claimed that he killed Saul. David grieved for the loss to his country and of his friend. Thus David was able to return home finally from exile. God, his Shepherd, had preserved and protected him through manifold events for years.

After returning to Judah David settled at Hebron. The leaders of Judah anointed him king of Judah at age thirty. Here he reigned seven and a half years. Then the elders of Israel, accompanied by a large army representing each of the tribes, came to Hebron and anointed David king of the nation. David captured Jerusalem which was destined to become the capitol of the nation. The Philistines now realized that David would be a serious threat and they attacked but he defeated them in several battles. Philistine domination of over Israel was over. His rule over Israel would be tested in many ways but the Lord was with him.

David desired to build a temple unto Jehovah his God but the Lord told Nathan that this was not His will. The reason God gave was that David had been such a man of war. The Lord promised David that one of his descendents would be allowed to build that temple in the future. David even received a divine promise that his descendants would reign on the throne forever; this evoked a glorious prayer of thanksgiving. The Lord's promise was fulfilled in the kingship of Jesus Christ. David's prayer and thanksgiving are recorded in 2 Samuel 7:18-29.

Scripture records after this that "the LORD preserved David whithersoever he went." During this time David wondered if there was anyone left in the house of Saul that he might show kindness for Jonathan's sake. This led to the discovery of the crippled Mephibosheth whom David took into his home and said that he would "eat bread always at my table." Thus he honored his friend.

There was a very dark and tragic episode in the life of King David. This occurred during a time when kings went forth to war but David sent Joab in his stead. This involved an incident one evening when David was walking on the roof of his home and he saw a woman bathing and she was beautiful to look upon; her name was Bathsheba. He inquired and found out who she was and sent messengers to bring her to him. He who had many wives took another man's wife for his pleasure that evening. This led to her conceiving a child; then David schemed to remedy the situation by ordering her husband Uriah, who was one of David's "mighty men" home from the battle. He hoped that as a result no one would suspect that the child was not Uriah's. However, Uriah refused to live with his wife while his military friends were exposed to death. David ordered him returned to the field of war and ordered Joab to put him in the most vulnerable place in the battle to insure his death. The honorable and mighty man was killed. After a period of mourning David took Bathsheba as his wife. The boy child was born. David's God sent His servant Nathan to the king and he told him a parable of a rich man who took his neighbor's one pet lamb to feed guests. David became angry and said, "As the LORD liveth, the man that hath done this thing shall surely die." God's man said to David, "Thou art the man!" The man of God rehearsed much that God had done for David through the years—"Now therefore the sword shall never depart from thine house; because thou hast despised me, and hast taken the wife of Uriah the Hittite to be thy wife. Thus saith the LORD, Behold, I will raise up evil against thee out of thine own house, and I will take thy wives before thine eyes, and give them unto thy neighbor, and he shall lie with thy wives in the sight of this sun." The king repented saying, "I have sinned against the LORD." In Psalm 51 he wrote in a much extended way of his repentance. David was reminded that he had given Jehovah's enemies an occasion to blaspheme. Nathan left David's house and Jehovah struck the child with sickness. David begged for the child's life but it died.

The non-departure of the sword from David's house was very evident in Amnon's forcing his half sister Tamar and after that he despised her; this led to Absalom, her brother, killing Amnon. Absalom ran away to his mother's country for three years. David wanted his son back and this was arranged by Joab. Absalom returned and began to wean the loyalty of the people away from David. This led to the full rebellion of Absalom. When he felt strong enough he gathered an army and had himself anointed king. Then he forced David to flee Jerusalem to a place east of the Jordan River. David now hit a low in his life. Even then David said, "Carry back the ark of God into the city: if I shall find favour in the eyes of the LORD, he will bring me again, and shew me both it, and his habitation: But if he thus say, I have no delight in thee; behold, here am I, let him do to me as seemeth good unto him."

Absalom's postponement of his attack gave David time to prepare with the result of the defeat and death of Absalom. Joab killed Absalom contrary to David's direct order which increased the tension in their relationship. There followed a time of turmoil. He was so angry at Joab that he chose Amasa as his replacement. Joab in turn killed Amasa. Sheba, who was of the tribe of Benjamin, Saul's tribe, rebelled and led the northern tribes against David but he was slain. Then came a three year famine that was observed as the judgment of God because of Saul's extermination of the Gibeonites. This led to David executing seven of Saul's sons but sparing Mephibosheth.

Then there was David's sin of numbering Israel. Once David realized how serious this sin was he confessed it to Jehovah. God used his prophet Gad to give a choice of three alternatives: [1] seven years of famine, [2] three months of military defeat or [3] three days of pestilence. David thought he could expect more mercy from God than at the hand of men so he chose the third alternative. Seventy-thousand people died in the pestilence, then Jerusalem was threatened David observed the angel of the Lord with a drawn sword and then he began to plead for mercy. God responded by staying the hand of judgment at that point. Gad instructed David to build an altar for worship.

The Philistines again fought against David in four battles and David's men killed four sons of the giant. This was the fulfillment of David's collecting five smooth stones and only using one of them for Goliath and the rest for his sons. David acknowledged his Great Shepherd as he presented his Song of Thanksgiving in 2 Samuel 22.[‡] David had been a man with many troubles, many enemies and much correction from the Lord. But as can be seen he could say joyfully, "My cup runneth over." There does not seem to be an exact period in David's life when he could have used all of the temporal expression that he makes in Psalm 23.

David, at the end of his earthly sojourn became ill. Even at the time of sickness his wife Haggith and his son Adonijah decided to take over the throne with the help of Joab. David's successor had already been selected and this was Solomon who was to be the next king. Upon hearing of the conspiracy David summoned Zadok the priest and Nathan the prophet to have a public anointing of Solomon. But the sword did not leave his house.

Solomon received instructions from his father on obeying the commandments of the Lord and building the temple out of the materials that he had collected for that purpose. After reigning in Jerusalem for thirty-three years David died at seventy and was buried in Jerusalem. We must weight Psalm 23 in the light of David's life. Clearly Psalm 23 is a gift from God delivered to us through the mind, heart and eyes of David as he was inspired by God the Holy Spirit.

[‡] See 2 Samuel 22.

Who could give an accurate account of the benefits of Psalm 23 to its readers?

There does not seem to be anyone who could account for perhaps millions who have refreshed themselves by these still waters. How often has this psalm been carried into places gripped with the greatest sorrow and there the voice of this psalm spoke to those who had ears to hear and hearts to receive its ministrations. Yes, in the dying hour or in the time of mourning for the dead its eloquence is clear and its comfort is abiding. Its message brings a pacifying "balm from Gilead" which when applied brings relief from sorrow's pain and healing in the midst of trouble. The real balm is applied by the great Physician-Shepherd our Lord Jesus Christ. If any man had knowledge of shepherding it was David the sweet Psalmist of Israel and the Holy Spirit used this to communicate to the children of grace.

This psalm is often instinctively turned into prayer: "Lord, would you be my shepherd; would you prevent me from suffering want; would you make me to lie down in green pastures; would you lead be beside the still waters where I may be refreshed; would you restore my soul; would you lead me in the paths of righteousness for your name's sake? Lord, when I walk through the valley of the shadow of death would you preserve me from evil; would you comfort me with the instruments of your Shepherdhood? Beloved Shepherd would you vindicate your truth which I believe before my enemies; would you anoint my head with the oil of consecration to you; would you cause this cup of your provision to continue to run over? Lord, oh that I would know your goodness and mercy all the days of my life and grant that I may dwell in your house forever." One of the Lord's servants wrote, "Our constant prayer ought therefore to be, that as we become older with every advancing moment, we may also become richer and riper in every heavenly grace."

While my Redeemer's near,
My shepherd and my guide,
I bid farewell to anxious fear,
My wants are all supplied.

To ever-fragrant meads,
Where rich abundance grows,
His gracious hand indulgent leads,
And guards, my sweet repose.

Along the lovely scene
Cool waters gently roll,
Transparent, sweet, and all serene,
To cheer my fainting soul.

Here let my spirit rest;
How sweet a lot is mine!
With pleasure, food, and safety blest;
Beneficence divine!

Dear Shepherd, if I stray,
My wandering feet restore;
To thy fair pastures guide my way,
And let me rove no more.

Unworthy as I am
Of thy protecting care,
Jesus, I plead thy gracious name,
For all my hopes are there.

-- Anne Steele (1716-1778)

Section 1

David Confessed: Jehovah-Jesus Is My Shepherd Therefore I Shall Not Want.

CHAPTER 1
The Lord Is My Shepherd

God the Holy Spirit led David to make his Confession in the language of his God given and youthful occupation as a shepherd of the family sheep. The lessons he learned as a shepherd boy would give the tenderest and most profound view of his relationship with the God of his salvation. David experienced the Lord in his life as seen in his confession: "The LORD is *my* shepherd." This he declared as he gave genuine utterance of his personal trust in Jehovah. David declared his identity with the LORD in various ways—"I will love thee, O LORD, *my* strength. The LORD is *my* rock, and *my* fortress, and *my* deliverer; *my* God, *my* strength, in whom I will trust; *my* buckler, and the horn of *my* salvation, and *my* high tower" (Ps. 18:1-2). Having Jehovah as his strength, fortress, deliverer, salvation and high tower gave David a sense of security whereby he prayed, "Hear the right, O LORD, attend unto *my* cry, give ear unto *my* prayer, that goeth not out of feigned [or hypocritical] lips. Let *my* sentence come forth from thy presence; let thine eyes behold the things that are equal" (Ps. 17:1-2).

The emphasis of David in his confession is the possessive pronoun "my." If this little word were removed or deleted the sense and sweetness of the entire psalm would be destroyed. Imagine David saying, "The Lord is *a*

Shepherd." The result would be a sense of incompleteness destroying the personal and experimental nature of Psalm 23. Without the personal aspect where would gratitude and joy find any room? However, no sooner had David said, "The LORD is *my* Shepherd," than his heart began to glow with gratitude and praise; then he triumphantly declared, "I shall not want," "I will fear no evil," and 'I will dwell in the house of the LORD forever." When faith grows in the heart it is expressed in words. David declared in another psalm, "The LORD is *my* light and *my* salvation; whom shall I fear? The LORD is the strength of *my* life; of whom shall I be afraid" (Ps. 27:1) or "I will love thee, O LORD, *my* strength" (Ps. 18:1) or "Thou art *my* God, and I will praise thee: thou art *my* God, I will exalt thee" (Ps. 118:28).

David began with his Shepherd Jehovah-Jesus. He knew God in His character as Shepherd which impacted David's heart of hearts. The point was not just a display of titles but the unfolding of the very person of God as Shepherd, as Salvation, as Fortress, as Deliverer, etc. He used the language of his early occupation to express the kind of trust in the LORD he enjoyed and the kind of care he received from the LORD. David knew the trust and dependence of his sheep and he had the same nature now by grace.

"This beautiful and instructive similitude informs us at once what the Lord is to the believer, and what the believer is to the Lord." And also "By this simple image David presents before us in a most graphic manner, the goodness, the tenderness, the watchful care, the providing love, the gracious nearness, and the protecting power, which God had manifested towards him," thus wrote John Stevenson.

David had an experiential sense of shepherding and he had a heart for sheep but he saw in his great God the ultimate Shepherd who would not nor could fail His sheep. This imagery gives the comfortable nature of his relationship with the great Jehovah. Since Jehovah was his Shepherd he had no sense of want; he had a sense of joyful rest and peace; he knew restoration and guidance; he had no fear of evil; he had comfort from his Shepherd's rod and staff; he had a table prepared for him in the presence of his enemies; he had the anointing of his Shepherd; he had a cup that was running over; he had goodness and mercy following him all the days of his life; he had the eternal prospect of dwelling in the House of the Lord forever. Thus he expressed the benefits and blessings that he and all of God's children experience as a result of the personification of the great Shepherd of the sheep.

Thus the Psalmist David in this Confession reflects on pictures of shepherding that brought comfort to his shepherding heart. Of course David had his Saviour Jehovah-Jesus in mind as his Shepherd. Yes, the infallible Shepherd is the object of David's trust. The very Shepherd who laid down His life for His sheep was the one and only in kind (John 10:11). David's pictures of the pastoral scene began with the sheep having satisfying green pastures, drinking from quiet still waters or peacefully lying down near those placid waters, when suddenly he refers to his Shepherd as refreshing his soul, guiding him in the path of righteousness. Even when he must walk through the valley of the shadow of death there is no fear of evil because his Shepherd-King is with him all the way to His house. His Shepherd's rod and staff did bring him a sense of comfort. He was even able to eat the food provided him by his

Shepherd even in his enemies presence. Next, his Shepherd-King anointed his head with oil and his cup ran over. His Shepherd-King so provided that only goodness and mercy could follow him throughout his life, but his final eternal home was in the house of Jehovah.

Yes, in this psalm David uses the imagery of shepherding. By divine inspiration he personifies the Shepherd and sheep. Only it is the Jehovah-Jesus who is the Shepherd with His flock under His care. In essence the Psalmist said, "I do not lack anything since Jehovah is my Shepherd."

What is the meaning of
"The LORD is my shepherd?"

Here is Jehovah-Jesus who is the Shepherd of the sheep. Psalm 23 has often been called *The Pearl of the Psalms* and *The Nightingale of the Psalms*. This psalm is an antidote for fear and describes *My Shepherd Jehovah-Jesus*! "Jehovah" is the Living One who is self-existent as the great I AM; it is He who was and is and is to come, who inhabits eternity whose name is Holy, who has life contained in Himself. "Jehovah" is the incommunicable name of the one who alone is Most High over all the earth (Ps. 83:18). This name signifies self-existence or existence without beginning or end. As "Jehovah" He is "the high and lofty One that inhabiteth eternity" (Isa. 57:15). Yes, He is the same one who is Alpha and Omega, the beginning and the end, who was, is and is to come, the almighty (Rev. 1:8). He has life in Himself (John 5:26); He gave life and breath to all things (Acts 17:25). Yes, He is the King eternal and the only wise God (1 Tim. 1:17), the everlasting God (Rom. 16:27), the same yesterday, today and forever (Heb. 13:8). The Shepherd of Israel leads Joseph like a flock and dwells between the cherubim (Ps. 80:1), He feeds his flock like a shepherd (Isa. 40:10-11). This is the Shepherd of whom Zechariah spoke (Zech. 13:7). This is the Jehovah that is David's Shepherd.

Thomas Watson, the Puritan preacher, in his sermon on "The Good Shepherd" from John 10:14 reminded: "Every line of Scripture has majesty shining in it. Jesus Christ is the very center of the gospel. If the Scripture is the field, Christ is the pearl in this field; and blessed is he who finds this pearl. The Scripture gives various descriptions of Christ. Sometimes He is called a Physician; He is the great Healer of souls; sometimes He is called a Captain. Hebrews 2:10: 'Captain of our salvation.' And here in the text He is a shepherd: 'I am the good Shepherd.' And this Shepherd has a flock; so it is in the text: 'I know my sheep, and am known of mine'" [*The Duty of Self-Denial*].

Christ Jesus is from the beginning of the world the only Shepherd of His sheep. He is the self-existing, uncreated, and eternal Jehovah; whose love, power and providence are unlimited and inexhaustible. His Shepherding care extends through all time, anticipates every emergency, comprehends every believer from the beginning of the world to the end, supplies their every need, and everlastingly secures the safety and happiness of every sheep in His flock. He is the all-sufficient Shepherd for in power He is almighty, in wisdom He is all-knowing, in love He is unequalled, and in resources He is without limit. Is there a danger He cannot foresee or avert? Is there an enemy He cannot subdue? Is there a need He cannot supply? His flock is different in age, desire, disposition, temptation and need, but He is capable of supplying their every need according to His riches in glory (Phil. 4:19). The eye of Jehovah-Jesus the Shepherd sees every facet of His flock, His ear is open to their bleating, and His hand administers to their need. When his sheep's heart is troubled He ministers peace, when weary He ministers rest, when penitent He ministers pardon, when hungry He ministers nourishment, when blind He gives sight, when sick He ministers healing, when weak He is their strength, when wavering He is their Rock, when tempted He is their deliverer, when confused He gives counsel, when lacking in understanding He gives wisdom, when guilty He grants forgiveness, when proud He clothes them in humility, when hasty He works patience, when insecure He enables them to persevere, and on their dying He bestows eternal life.

Christ Jesus is the *Good Shepherd*: Jesus said, "I am the *good shepherd*: the *good shepherd* giveth his life for the sheep.... I am the *good shepherd*, and know my sheep, and am known of mine." Actually *"good"* has the sense of worthiness or excellency and thus it could be translated *Worthy Shepherd.* "As the Father knoweth me, even so know I the Father: and I lay down my life for the sheep. And other sheep I have, which are not of this fold: them also I must bring, and they shall hear my voice; and there shall be one fold, and *one shepherd*" (John 10:11, 14-16; we need to expand on this passage later).

He is the *Great Shepherd*: "Now the God of peace, that brought again from the dead our Lord Jesus, that *great shepherd* of the sheep, through the blood of the everlasting covenant, Make you perfect in every good work to do his will, working in you that which is well pleasing in his sight, through Jesus Christ; to whom be glory for ever and ever. Amen" (Heb. 13:20-21). This *Great Shepherd* made the sheep, claimed the sheep, redeemed the sheep and eternally secures the sheep.

Christ Jesus is the *Shepherd-Bishop*: "For ye were as sheep going astray; but are now returned unto the *Shepherd* and *Bishop* of your souls" (1 Pet. 2:25). "All we like sheep have gone astray" (Isa. 53:6). The Lord's sheep were once wanderers from Him, but the Lord Jesus as Shepherd-Bishop retrieved them in grace. "Your conscience is the diocese where none may visit but Christ. Christ is called in Scripture 'the chief shepherd of all'" [Thomas Watson]. Jesus is the *Chief Shepherd*: "And when the *chief Shepherd* shall appear, ye shall receive a crown of glory that fadeth not away" (1 Pet. 5:4).

Jesus will be the eternal *Lamb-Shepherd*: "for the Lamb which is in the midst of the throne shall feed them [or shall be their shepherd], and shall lead them unto living fountains of waters: and God shall wipe away all tears from their eyes" (Rev. 7:17). Yes, we need this Lamb-Shepherd!

Jehovah-Jesus is well known in the Bible. "Behold, the Lord GOD will come with strong hand, and his arm shall rule for him: behold, his reward is with him, and his work before him. He shall feed his flock *like a shepherd*: he shall *gather the lambs* with his arm, and carry them in his bosom, and shall gently lead those that are with young" (Isa. 40:10-11). What does He do for the sheep? "All we like sheep have gone astray; we have turned every one to his own way; and the LORD hath laid on him the iniquity of us all" (Isa. 53:6); therefore He was the substitutionary sacrifice for His sheep. He saves them all and not one of them is lost.

What a glorious theme is the shepherd-sheep pictured in God's Word. It is a consoling picture of the tending of sheep in the pasture and the shepherd's watch care of his flock. Oh, how the Lord has blessed His people in this portrayal with which they may identify.

Seven of Jehovah's names are found in essence in this Psalm:

Jehovah-Rohi—"The LORD is my shepherd" (Ps. 23:1).

Jehovah-Jireh—The LORD will provide—"I shall not want" (v. 1).

Jehovah-Shalom—The LORD is peace—"He leadeth me beside the still waters" (v. 2).

Jehovah-Rophi—The LORD heals—"He restoreth my soul" v. 3).

Jehovah-Tsidkenu—The LORD our righteousness—"He leadeth me in the paths of righteousness" (v. 3).

Jehovah-Shammah—The LORD is there—"Thou art with me" (v. 4).

Jehovah-Nissi—The LORD my banner—"Thou prepares a table before me in the presence of mine enemies" (v. 5).

Think of this 23rd Psalm which introduces us [1] to the person of the Shepherd (v. 1), [2] to the provision of the Shepherd (v. 2), [3] to the pathway provided by the Shepherd (v. 3), [4] to the presence in peril of the Shepherd (v. 4), [5] to the preparation made by the Shepherd (v. 5) and [6] to the prospect because of the Shepherd (v. 6).

There are three major results that David discloses as a result of his "Confession." [1] Jehovah-Jesus is My Shepherd therefore I shall not want, [2] Jehovah-Jesus is My Shepherd therefore I will fear no evil, and [3] Jehovah-Jesus is My Shepherd therefore I shall dwell in His house forever. This is a very personal and God centered psalm for the psalmist refers to himself seventeen times and to

Jehovah thirteen times. The greatness of this Shepherd results in "I shall not want," "I will fear no evil" and "I will dwell in the house of the LORD forever." These three declarations by the Psalmist unfold in Psalm 23 for us! Since this is true I shall not lack, I shall not be afraid and I shall have an eternal home!

Isaac Watts did a three part version of this psalm in his Psalter. The second part states,

> My Shepherd will supply my need,
> Jehovah is his name;
> In pastures fresh He makes me feed,
> Beside the living stream.
>
> He brings my wandering spirit back,
> When I forsake his ways,
> And leads me, for his mercy's sake,
> In paths of truth and grace.
>
> When I walk through the shades of death
> Thy presence is my stay;
> One word of thy supporting breath
> Drives all my fears away.
>
> Thy hand, in sight of all my foes,
> Doth still my table spread;
> My cup with blessings overflows,
> Thine oil anoints my head.
>
> The sure provisions of my God
> Attend me all my days;
> O may thy house be mine abode,
> And all my work be praise!

There would I find a settled rest,
While others go and come,
No more a stranger or a guest,
But like a child at home.

"The Lord is my shepherd; I shall not want." Please consider [1] what that does not mean; [2] what does that mean; and [3] why that is true.

What does "I shall not want" *not* mean? The children of this world grasp at shadows and have no idea of what true riches look like, for they are spiritually blind. They do not know the true Shepherd; Him they do not recognize. Remember our Lord Jesus was always poor by man's standards for He wore hand-me-down clothes and had nowhere to lay His head. He never sought other than His Father's will and never worked wonders to satisfy His hunger. The Psalmist is not referring primarily to outward circumstance. David is not saying that he expects great affluence and abundance to always be provided. No! He does not presume on Jehovah-Jesus; he does not presume to predetermine what his own earthly blessings should be. What is he saying? His Shepherd has his confidence because His pastoral care will do him good and not evil. His Shepherd's credentials are impeccable. He is saying his Shepherd will maintain His promise that all things are working for the good of those who love God and are called according to His purpose (Romans 8:28). David believes that the enemies, the needs, the problems, the circumstances will be met by his Shepherd who does all things well.

What does "I shall not want" mean? What a declaration is "I shall not want!" David is saying I shall not lack anything spiritually, materially, physically or mentally. Why is that true? This Shepherd is Jehovah-Jesus! Thus David speaks of his own position as a member of the most prized flock in existence which is shepherded by the Almighty who is the All-sufficient Shepherd. With such a Shepherd how could we lack what He wants for us? Since we have such a Shepherd, *Jehovah-rohi*, we shall not want because we desire our All-sufficient Shepherd's will. What He wants for us is what we need for He knows best! "You tell me that a godly man wants these and these things, which the wicked man has; but I tell you he can no more be said to '*want*' them than a butcher may be said to want Homer, or another thing, because his disposition is such, that he makes no use of those things which you usually mean. 'Tis but only necessary things that he cares for, and those are not many. But *one* thing is necessary, and that he has chosen, namely, *the better part*" [Zachary Bogan].

We trust our Shepherd to do right for He also takes care of sparrows, ravens and the hairs on our head. This Shepherd has provided what was necessary to our spiritual wellbeing, mental-emotional wellbeing, moral-social wellbeing and earthly-material needs. Remember what John's quote of Jesus, "I am the *good or worthy shepherd*: *the good or worthy shepherd* giveth his life *for* the sheep" (John 10:11). Here is the Shepherd with the ultimate concern and care expressed in self-sacrifice. His death was in the stead of His sheep. "The death of the Shepherd is the life of the sheep" [Thomas Watson]. Here the word "for" means "in behalf of" showing that Jesus gave Himself as a substitutionary sacrifice for His sheep; He substituted

Himself in their place; He bore their sins and He imputed to them His righteousness. The sheep do not lack a sin bearer, a saviour, a worthy shepherd for Jesus paid it all. John went on quoting Jesus, "I am the *good shepherd*, and know my sheep, and am known of mine" (John 10:14). Not only did Jesus pay the sin debt but He knows or loves His sheep and they reciprocate toward Him. Then Jesus continued, "As the Father knoweth me, even so know I the Father: and I lay down my life for the sheep. And other sheep I have, which are not of this fold: them also I must bring, and they shall hear my voice; and there shall be one fold, and *one shepherd*" (John 10:15-16). There are sheep that are from the Gentiles as well as from the Jews. These effectually "hear" His voice and become part of "one fold." Jesus calls His own sheep "by name, and leadeth them out" (John 10:3). He knows all about His sheep in thought, word and deed. Thomas Watson said this Shepherd "sets a double mark upon His sheep. One is the earmark of election. 'I have chosen you,' He said; and besides that he has set another mark upon His sheep. He seals them by His Spirit, Ephesians 4:30." The Holy Spirit seals them "unto the day of redemption." Jesus secures His sheep by asking His Father to keep them, sanctify them and requested they be with Him where He is (John 17:15, 17, 24).

Why do we not want? Our Shepherd Jehovah-Jesus has taken a personal interest in providing for us. How? He declared, "I lay down my life for the sheep" (John 10:15, 11) for His substitutionary sacrifice shows the extent of His love; "Therefore doth my Father love me, because I lay down my life, that I might take it again. No man taketh it from me, but I lay it down of myself" (John 10:17-18). Our Shepherd made a willing sacrifice. He was "led as a sheep to the slaughter." He insisted, "I know them [my sheep] and they follow me: And I give unto them eternal life; and they shall never perish, neither shall any man pluck them out of my hand. My Father, which gave them me, is greater than all; and no man is able to pluck them out of my Father's hand" (John 10:27-28). This is why His sheep "shall not want." Read that glorious passage in Isaiah 53. Obadiah Sedgwick, another Puritan, said our Shepherd provides for our conditions but not our corruptions.

There is an account of one of the Lord's sheep who seemed to be in a pitiable condition, but was enabled by the Spirit of grace to remain cheerfully dependant on God. He was poor and greatly reduced in his earthly circumstances. During his old age he did not murmur over his poverty. One day a neighbor said to him, "You must be bad off and I don't know how you and your wife can continue to maintain yourself." His reply was "I have a rich Father, and He does not allow me to be in want." The neighbor asserted, "Has your father not died yet! He must be very old." "Oh," he said, "my Father never dies, and He always takes care of me!" This aged Christian's struggles with poverty were well known to others. Then as old age removed the old fellows ability to work the Lord had charity extended to him. He would often go forth from his scanty breakfast not knowing where his next meal would come from but his faith continued. With David he replied regarding his Shepherd's care, "I shall not want." Our Shepherd responds to faith. Unbelief is a difficult taskmaster for Jehovah-Jesus the Shepherd "did not many mighty works there [in His own country and in His own house], because of their unbelief" (Matt. 13:58).

Are you a contented sheep? Remember Paul's words to Timothy from Sacred Scripture, "But godliness with contentment is great gain. For we brought nothing into this world, and it certain we can carry nothing out. And having food and raiment let us be therewith content" (1 Tim. 6:6-8). With such a Shepherd His sheep can be contented. Our Shepherd provides what is needed for each sheep of His flock and he knows each sheep by name. Thus the sheep should say, "I shall not want." When we call Jesus our Shepherd and don't believe He will provide for us this reflects on His faithfulness. Do we live in the light of His goodness or in the darkness of mistrust? David sought to trust the help of his Shepherd when the lion and bear attacked, but he also did so when attacked by the giant. David could have spoken the words of Paul, "Not that I speak in respect of want: for I have learned, in whatsoever state I am, therewith to be content. I know both how to be abased, and I know how to abound: every where and in all things I am instructed both to be full and to be hungry, both to abound and to suffer need. I can do all things through Christ which strengtheneth me" (Phil. 4:11-13). Since Jehovah-Jesus is my Shepherd, "I shall not want." Remember Jesus' words, "Therefore take no thought, saying, What shall we eat? Or, What shall we drink? Or, Wherewithal shall we be clothed? ... for your heavenly father knoweth that ye have need of all these things" (Matt. 6:31-32). Do you trust Him for the greatest need that is the spiritual one? Have you embraced the Lamb of God as your Savior from sin by faith? The Shepherd sees to all the needs of His flock.

In what position shall this Shepherd's sheep not want? They shall not want upwardly, downwardly, inwardly, backwardly, forwardly, onwardly and foreverly.

[1] As a true believer I can look *upward* and declare, "I shall not want," for Jehovah-Jesus is my Shepherd. He sits on the Fathers right hand as victor over death, hell and the grave; and all power in heaven and in earth is given Him. There He intercedes for His sheep.

[2] As a true believer I can look *downward* and declare, "I shall not want," for Jehovah-Jesus is my Shepherd. This earth upon which I live was created by Him and redeemed by Him. He still clothes the lilies of the field, provides for the birds of the air, for the fish of the sea, for the beasts of the field, etc. He declares to me "I shall not want."

[3] As a true believer I can look *inward* and declare, "I shall not want," for Jehovah-Jesus is my Shepherd. He has put spiritual life in me along with a heavenly hope. He has provided me with an abhorrence of sin and a hunger for righteousness. He has given me ears to hear His voice as my Shepherd and my feet desire to follow Him.

[4] As a true believer I can look *backward* and declare, "I shall not want," for Jehovah-Jesus is my Shepherd. He preserved me in the past and will unto the day of salvation. Although I am unworthy He loved me ere I knew Him. When I was yet a sinner Jesus Christ died for me.

[5] As a true believer I can look *forward* and declare, "I shall not want," for Jehovah-Jesus is my Shepherd. The future trials and troubles my Shepherd has made certain promises regarding, "as my day is so my strength shall be." He has said, "Be content with such things as ye have: for he hath said, I will never leave thee nor forsake thee" (Heb. 13:5). He will say, "Come, ye blessed of my Father, inherit

47

the kingdom prepared for you from the foundation of the world" (Matt. 25:34).

[6] As a true believer I can look *onward* and *forever* and declare, "I shall not want," for Jehovah-Jesus is my Shepherd. My Shepherd has provided the removal of all my sin, the victory over every enemy, the deliverance of the kingdom to my Father and God who is all in all! The believer can gaze *outward* and *onward* and *eternally heavenward* exclaiming with wonder, thanksgiving and adoration, "I shall *never* want!" Yes, come and inherit the kingdom prepared for you from the foundation of the world. Enter into the joys of the Lord.

In Psalm 23 David describes some major areas for which the sheep are provided. This Shepherd's sheep have nothing to worry about for everything is within the scope of His omnipotent power and omniscient will. Therefore the present and future are sovereignly moderated.

CHAPTER 2
I Shall Not Want:
Because He Makes Me Lie Down in Green Pastures

I shall not want because He makes provision for His sheep. "He maketh me to lie down in green pastures" (v. 2a). This seems to emphasize the need for rest and refreshment. What a scene is opened to our view as we begin verse 2. Here is indeed a pastoral scene of the Shepherd making provision for His sheep. It is the Shepherd who is superintending the flock; it is "He." David as it were is giving an eyewitness account as he observes his Saviour Shepherd who made him a member of His flock— "He maketh me." David is telling us what the Shepherd is doing for him. The Psalmist was not making an idle boast when he affirmed, "I shall not want." The love and care of the Shepherd, David has personally experienced. Before us is pictured the *posture* of the sheep and the *pasture* for the sheep.

Shepherds have described the natural shepherd / sheep relationship, so consider the following scene: the sheep are grazing from around sunrise until late morning; then they rest by lying down for around three to four hours and they began to chew their cuds. Thus they are doing what enhances their health and increases their body weight. A good shepherd will promote this schedule and if possible find a shade in which they may rest. This is the routine that provides for contentment. "Green pastures" has a sense of tender grass which provides not just food but a soft bed midst cool refreshment. This is a unique condition in a land of extremes in climate.

David was expressing that his Shepherd had already brought him into the experience of spiritual privileges that were nourishing and sustaining him. Therefore he can compare himself to a sheep that was lying down in "green pastures." The marginal translation note has it, "pastures of tender grass." This provision is at its most succulent stage. This is the way David presents a metaphor for the prime spiritual provision which the Shepherd had made for His eternal sheep. All credit is given to the Shepherd for "He maketh me" and this is as if David had said, "My Shepherd's care is such that without Him I would not have found the pastures green. Therefore, without His kindness, care and protection I would never enjoy this abundance of provision and lie down in a state of spiritual rest."

David's point deals with the *pasture* and the *posture*. His reference to the *pasture* points to abundance of supply, the maximum quality and the nutrition needed. Then he reflects on the *posture* of lying down in that succulent pasture which was representative of the spiritual rest and peace to which he was accommodated by grace. One point to be remembered is that the pasture is more than sufficient for all the flock.

Consider what is most important here: the spiritual relationship of Jehovah-Jesus to His sheep. Here we are to grasp the intervention of our Shepherd in our lives for our good. David is pointing to the Shepherd making us to lie down as metaphorically representing those dwelling secure with provision and peace. Because of the self-sacrifice of our Lord Jesus He has provided spiritual peace and refreshment for His sheep feeding them upon His Word. The pasture is of God's nourishing Word. His Word is eternal, "For ever, O LORD, thy word is settled in heaven" (Ps. 119:89). Thankfully we have an unchanging promise from our Worthy Shepherd.

Are we resting upon the promises of that eternal Word as the sheep lying down in green grass and chewing the cud? The pastures are of tender grass with sheep grazing, which points to the fields of Scriptures. God's Word is the only depositary of eternal truth and our blessed Saviour-Shepherd had declared that "man shall not live by bread alone, but by every word that proceedeth out of the mouth of God" (Matt. 4:4).

There is an adversary that the Shepherd must protect the flock from and that is the devil, who is actively opposed—"He was a murderer from the beginning, and abode not in the truth, because there is no truth in him. When he speaketh a lie, he speaketh of his own: for he is a liar, and the father of it" (John 8:44). This enemy of the flock is like a roaring lion seeking to destroy. Our Shepherd preserves His sheep in life and for eternity, for He said, "And this is life eternal, that they might know thee the only true God, and Jesus Christ, whom thou hast sent. I have glorified thee on the earth: I have finished the work which thou gavest me to do" (John 17:3-4). The tender grass for sheep is not found anywhere but in the Scriptures. "Search the Scriptures; for in them ye think ye have eternal life: and they are they which testify of me" (John 5:39). This Word of our Shepherd is a life giving Word which is able to make us wise unto salvation through faith in Christ Jesus (2 Tim. 3:17).

An ancient divine said, "The holy Bible is a spiritual paradise, and the book of Psalms is the tree of life in the midst!" Another wrote of the pasture of tender grass, "In the holy Scriptures are doctrines most divine—prophecies most certain—laws most holy, just and good—covenants betwixt God and man, most gracious—promises, most precious— privileges, most ample—providences, most wonderful— ordinances, most comfortable and soul reviving: here whatsoever is taught is truth—whatsoever is commanded is good—whatsoever is promised is happiness!"

The tender grass of the Word is also pictured as a tree of life baring twelve kinds of fruits and yielding fruit every month, and its leaves are for the healing of the nations (Rev. 22:2). The Word of our Shepherd is the well of truth; only faith has the vessel to draw out its refreshing waters. It is a mirror in which we behold the almighty God in His beloved Son as the forgiver of sin and the reconciler of sinners. In the tender grass of Scripture alone can be found perfect truth—sure promises—the most gracious invitation—and the wisest counsel. Herein is praise without flattery— reproof without harshness—and love without end. What is the quality of this tender grass? "The words of the LORD are pure words" (Ps. 12:6). What does the Word provide for the sheep? If the sheep is a stranger here is his citizenship; if he is a pilgrim here is his staff; if he is a traveler here is his guide; if he is on a voyage here is his chart; if he is a soldier here is his spiritual armor: the shield of faith, the sword of the Spirit, the girdle of truth, the breastplate of righteousness and the helmet of salvation. Whatever the sheep needs is provided herein: food when he is hungry, water when he is thirsty, medicine when he is sick, and a cordial when he is faint. Whatever the circumstances the sheep experiences the Word of God is as "green pastures" to his soul (read Psalm 19:7-11)! Our Shepherd said, "Heaven and earth shall pass away: but my words shall not pass away" (Mark 13:31). Our path is illuminated by His Word (Ps. 119:105). Jesus our Shepherd provides the climate for spiritual refreshment, "Peace I leave with you, my peace I give unto you: not as the world giveth, give I unto you. Let not your heart be troubled, neither let it be afraid" (John 14:27). There is the sense of security in Christ our Shepherd.

Another consideration here is the fact that these are "green pastures" of the preached Word in the Lord's House. Thus David said, "I was glad when they said unto me, Let us go into the house of the LORD.... Because of the house of the LORD our God I will seek thy good" (Ps. 122:1, 9). "How amiable are thy tabernacles, O LORD of hosts! My soul longeth, yea, even fainteth for the courts of the LORD: my heart and my flesh crieth out for the living God" (Ps. 84:1-2). One has written, "It is the presence of the Lord in His church, in His Word, and in His ordinances, by the Holy Spirit, that makes them green pastures to the soul." The Shepherd of the sheep causes His sheep to "lie down" in those green pastures. Thus their hunger has been appeased, their wants have been satisfied, and they can now be at rest. This is the glorious position of the sheep or the believer in Christ. The green pastures of the Spiritual Shepherd satisfies the soul—"My soul shall be satisfied as with marrow and fatness; and my mouth shall praise thee with joyful lips: When I remember thee upon my bed, and meditate on thee in the night watches" (Ps. 63:5-6).

Those who "lie down in green pastures" are those chewing the cud or meditating. The ruminating over the food that had been provided and eaten is chewed over by the sheep as he rests. As sheep chew the cud so the believer thinks over the Word of God in his mind as he continues to reflect on its meaning and application. We also speak to ourselves in psalms, hymns and spiritual songs (Eph. 5:19). Meditation is a privilege and a duty of the believer-sheep. It is the holy and healthful chewing of spiritual food to enjoy its ultimate value. Oh, to contemplate and meditate on the Word of God. Daily meditation and prayer are a preservative to having a healthy soul. Studying to show ourselves approved of God. The hearing of the proclamation of the Scriptures is a comparison to chewing or meditating. The Shepherd led His sheep to a luxuriant place not only for lying down but for the purpose of drawing near to Him (1 Sam. 14:36). David practiced meditating, "O how love I thy law! It is my meditation all the day.... How sweet are thy words unto my taste! yea, sweeter than honey to my mouth" (Ps. 119:97, 103)! We shall thus be satisfied with the goodness of God's house (Ps. 65:4).

The Shepherd brought the sheep to experience green pastures. While there they received the benefits of the tender grass and then they lay down in those pastures to review as it were the food they had eaten. Yes, they chewed the cud which could be perceived as a form of giving thanks as well as meditation. Remember Jesus' words of invitation to His sheep, "Come unto me, all ye that labour and are heavy laden, and I will give you rest" (Matt. 11:28). Oh, how delightful for the sheep after being worn by the cares and anxieties of life to retire to those green pastures! Sheep need to rest in their Shepherd because of who He is:

Jesus, I am resting, resting
In the joy of what thou art;
I am finding out the greatness
Of thy loving heart.

Thou hast bid me gaze upon thee,
As thy beauty fills my soul,
For by thy transforming power,
Thou hast made me whole.

Jesus, I am resting, resting
In the joy of what thou art;
I am finding out the greatness
Of thy loving heart.

O how great thy lovingkindness,
Vaster, broader than the sea!
O how marvelous thy goodness
Lavished all on me!
Yes, I rest in thee, Beloved,
Know what wealth of grace is thine,
Know thy certainty of promise
And have made it mine.

The Pastor-Shepherd welcomes His troubled sheep to His pastures of green. "I will feed my flock, and I will cause them to lie down, saith the Lord GOD" (Ez. 34:15). Thus the sheep have every provision. F. B. Meyer in his *Our Daily Homily* commented on this text:

It is perfectly impossible to make sheep lie down unless they are satisfied or free from alarm. When the flocks lie deep in the rich pasture lands, it is because they have eaten to the full, and are quiet from fear of evil. When, therefore, the shepherd and bishop of our souls promises that he will so deal with us as to cause us to lie down, he undertakes to fulfill in our life these two conditions.

The Lord Jesus brings us into a good pasture, and causes us to feed in a fat pasture upon the mountains of fellowship, transfiguration, and far reaching vision. Listen as he cries, 'Eat, yea, eat abundantly, oh beloved.' Our restlessness arises from our refusal to obey his loving invitation to come and dine. We do not read our Bibles enough.... Let us look at scripture as the green pastures; and as we open them let us ask him to be our guide, and to show us where the food appropriate to our need is to be found.

The Lord Jesus does more. He makes with us a covenant of peace; and even if the evil beasts do not cease out of the land, he so assures us that we can dwell safely in the wilderness and sleep in the woods. He intends that we should be safe in Immanuel's land; that the bonds of our yoke should be broken; and that we should be delivered out of the hands of those who serve themselves of us.

Oh child of God, be less dependent on people and circumstances! Deal more constantly at first hand with Jesus. Regard him as your shepherd; 'He maketh to lie down.' Rejoice that he the Lord your God is with you....

Our Shepherd said, "Lo, I come: in the volume of the book it is written of me" (Ps. 40:7). The Volume of Truth is filled with our Shepherd for it is His green pastures for His flock. Are you resting in Him, in His provision, in His providence, in His pasture, in His peace? Are His green pastures your desire? Remember in this state to give thanks and meditate upon what your Shepherd has told you. As you read His Word do you reflect and think upon it after having read it as a message of you Shepherd to you? Remember Isaac "went out to meditate in the field at the eventide" (Gen. 24:63). David declared, "I will remember the works of the LORD: surely I will remember thy wonders of old. I will meditate also of all thy work, and talk of thy doings" (Ps. 77:11-12). Paul's words to Timothy were, "Till I come, give attendance to reading, to exhortation, to doctrine.... Meditate upon these things; give thyself wholly to them; that thy profiting may appear to all" (1 Tim. 4:13, 15).

When did you last obey your Shepherd in lying down in green pastures? Let the inspired Word of God be your daily study, be your devotional truth, be your delight and be for your diligent meditation. Every verse has something to say to you from the Lord your Shepherd so as to prevent wanting. Do you take the position of the Psalmist? "I will sing unto the LORD as long as I live: I will sing praise to my God while I have my being. My meditation of him shall be sweet: I will be glad in the LORD" (Ps. 104:33-34).

Our Shepherd says of those who are not of His sheep, "This is the rest wherewith ye may cause the weary to rest; and this is the refreshing: yet they would not hear. But the word of the LORD was unto them precept upon precept, precept upon precept; line upon line, line upon line; here a little, and there a little; that they might go, and fall backward, and be broken, and snared, and taken" (Isa. 28:12-13). Jesus said, "My sheep hear my voice, and I know them, and they follow me: And I give unto them eternal life; and they shall never perish, neither shall nay man pluck them out of my hand" (John 10:27-28). What a Shepherd! His sheep "did all eat the same spiritual meat" (1 Cor. 10:3).

CHAPTER 3
I Shall Not Want:
Because He Leads Me Beside Still Waters

I shall not want because He leads me beside still waters. The sheep can say, "He leadeth me beside the still waters" (v. 2b). From the natural shepherd/sheep relationship shepherds know that sheep do not like to drink from gurgling or rushing water. There are many small springs high in the hills whose waters run down the valleys only to evaporate under the desert sun. Although the sheep need the water, they prefer not to drink from fast-flowing streams because of the danger it instinctively imposes; if their wool becomes wet they sink and drown. The shepherd must find a place where rocks or erosion have made a little pool, or else fashion with the hands, a place to hold water; the pool needs to sufficiently hold at least a few gallons. Let us now go from the natural realm of sheep to the spiritual realm of the Lord's sheep. The word translated "leadeth" has a sense of gentle leading. This is the way the Lord cares for His people. He is merciful and longsuffering in His leading.

There are certain areas that are essential for the prolonging of the life of the sheep. The Shepherd's task is to see to the meeting of their needs. "I shall not want" for *food* because "He maketh me to lie down in green pastures." "I shall not want" for *drink* because "He leadeth me beside the still waters." Our Shepherd leads His sheep beside the still waters because He knows the *nature* and the *need* of His sheep? By *nature* a sheep must be led and cared for in a certain way. By *need* a sheep must have water that is accessible without the fear of drowning. Thirst is the most essential of all natural needs and a good shepherd seeks to meet that need to prevent the dehydration and death of His sheep; therefore he keeps them near a source of water which is critical in an arid or hostile country.

The sheep are moved from pasture to pasture to insure their proper feeding. However, he always keeps in mind areas that provide water in case one spring or water source dries up. David was well aware of these needs for as a shepherd he had to keep these matters before his mind. Thus when David now speaks of His Shepherd his experience is that "He leadeth me beside the still waters." He is the great and unfailing provider. These are waters conducive to satisfaction of the thirst, rest and quietness.

Water, of course, is an essential element in maintaining physical life just as God the Holy Spirit is the imparter of and maintainer of spiritual life. The work of regeneration or the new birth, which is the impartation of eternal life, is the work of God the Holy Spirit based on Christ's atonement and the Father's choice. The Shepherd through the Spirit is engaged in leading His flock safely to the heavenly Canaan. This world is filled with dangers through which they must be conducted. There are arid deserts, barren hills, dark forests, rocky mountains, narrow defiles, dry streams and at times scant shelter. Thankfully our Shepherd maintains the utmost personal care, a most vigilant watch and a supreme power to preserve His sheep to their journey's end. He has declared and assured that not one of them is lost (John 17:12; 18:9). Their providential care is beside "still waters." When the way becomes rough "He carries the lambs in His bosom, and gently leads those that are with young" (Isa. 40:11). However, He never suffers them to be too far from the refreshing water.

Our Shepherd's sheep "shall drink of the brook in the way: therefore shall he lift up the head" (Ps. 110:7). The conquest of life is such that there are periodic needs for satisfying the thirst. Gideon gathered an army of his countrymen to go out to war against the Midianites on the Plain of Jezreel. He wanted some assurance from the Lord that he was the man for the job and ask for a fleece test (Judges 6:36-40). Gideon's army was too big in God's estimation, there were 32,000; there was not to be any misplaced understanding on who gave the victory, yea, no bragging on the arm of flesh. Thus the Lord whittled the number down to 300. The soldiers were tested twice more by the Lord: when He sent the fearful home it still left too many, so they were tested again by the way they took water (Judges 7).

Thus the sheep shall be refreshed during their lives by the great Shepherd from the brook in the way. Remember when Samson was in need, "And he was sore athirst, and called on the LORD, and said, Thou hast given this great deliverance into the hand of thy servant: and now shall I die for thirst, and fall into the hand of the uncircumcised? But God clave an hollow place that was in the jaw, and there came water thereout; and when he had drunk, his spirit came again, and he revived: wherefore he called the name thereof Enhakkore [meaning fountain of him who cried],

61

which is in Lehi unto this day" (Judges 15:18-19). With great victory Samson is reminded to not trust in the flesh for his intense thirst was like everyone else's for he was mortal. He needed a drink of water by the way and Jehovah provided it in a most unique way.

Remember how the Lord led Elijah during the great time of draught and he drank from the brook and was fed by ravens (1 Kings 17:1-7); then when that brook in God's providence dried up the Lord sent him to a widow who had a source of water (17:8-16). After the supply of water from the Shepherd they may lift up their heads refreshed. One of the Lord's servants said, "This placid stream flows ever parallel with the path of righteousness; and, as that path winds onward, its current also winds, and with each turning of the road flows gently forward. Should any member of the flock deviate from the appointed path, he would soon bitterly experience that he had lost sight of the stream of peace. The insatiable thirst within, no other waters could assuage. So long, however, as he followed in the footsteps of the good Shepherd, so long would he have reason to acknowledge, with a grateful heart, that he invariably led him beside the still waters" [John Stevenson].

The worthy Shepherd guides and is assisted by the Holy Spirit or the Comforter; Jesus has the Father sent to also lead "beside the still waters or the waters of quietness or the waters of rest." Thus the Comforter has come according to faithful promise of the Shepherd (John 15:26-27). Every divine provision He makes for His sheep. Remember that on "that great day of the feast, Jesus stood and cried, saying, If any man thirst, let him come unto me, and drink. He that believeth on me, as the scripture hath said, out of his belly shall flow rivers of living water. (But this spake he of the Spirit, which they that believe on him should receive: for the Holy Ghost was not yet given; because that Jesus was not yet glorified)" (John 7:37-39). The Shepherd provides for His thirsty sheep, that they "Therefore with joy shall ... draw water out of the wells of salvation" (Isa. 12:3). The still waters from our Shepherd are satisfying. Remember Jesus' words to the Samaritan woman at the well? "Jesus answered and said unto her, Whosoever drinketh of this water shall thirst again: But whosoever drinketh of the water that I shall give him shall never thirst; but the water that I shall give him shall be in him a well of water springing up into everlasting life" (John 4:13-14). Our Shepherd invites His sheep to this water, "Ho, every one that thirsteth, come ye to the waters, and he that hath no money; come ye, buy, and eat; yea, come, buy wine and milk without money and without price" (Isa. 55:1). John Calvin explained,

> Here the Prophet describes in lofty terms of commendation the goodness of God, which was to be poured down more copiously and abundantly than before under the reign of Christ, 'in whose hand are hid all the treasures' (Col. 2:3) of the grace of God; for in him God fully explains his mind to us; so that the saying of John is actually fulfilled, 'We have all drawn from his fullness, and have received grace for grace' (John 1:16).... But he hath poured it out far more liberally and abundantly in Christ. Thus, it is a remarkable commendation of the grace of God, which is exhibited to us in the kingdom of Christ; for the Prophet does not instruct us what has been done once, but also what is done every day, while the Lord invites us by his doctrine to the enjoyment of all blessings. *Come to the waters.*

Some view the word 'waters' as referring to the doctrine of the Gospel, and others to the Holy Spirit; but neither of these expositions, in my opinion, is correct. They who think that it denotes the doctrine of the Gospel, and who contrast it with the law, include only one part of what the Prophet meant. They who expound it as denoting the Holy Spirit have somewhat more plausibility, and quote that passage of John's Gospel, 'If thou knewest the gift of God, and who it is that saith to thee, Give me to drink, thou wouldest have asked of him, and he would have given thee living water' (John 4:10).

David spoke in the plural—"He leadeth me beside the still waters." As has already been seen there are different kinds of waters. Jesus told the woman at the well about water that was "living water" (John 4:11-15). Every effort is expended by our Shepherd to provide what His sheep need. Sadly the sheep can stray and deprive themselves of the Shepherd's consoling refreshment by their sin. The Shepherd is always watchful of His sheep lest they turn to forbidden cisterns and seek relief where it never can be found. The sheep He leads by outward circumstances and by the inward guidance and instruction of the Holy Spirit. The Spirit quenches their spiritual thirst at the streams of Divine truth. Oh what a reviving the waters bring to the fainting soul when the Spirit gives them to drink of the water of everlasting promises! The Shepherd pours forth living waters from the eternal fountain for His sheep and they become a "well of water, springing up unto everlasting life" (John 4:14).

The living water has been provided by our Shepherd. So why are you thirsty? Can you say with David, "As the hart panteth after the water brooks, so panteth my soul after thee, O God; my soul thirsteth for God, for the living God" (Ps. 42:1-2). Have you been to the forbidden cisterns seeking water that cannot satisfy the thirst? Is David's cry your cry, "my soul thirsteth for thee, my flesh longeth for thee in a dry and thirsty land, where no water is" (Ps. 63:1). We are living in a spiritual desert so we are in need of the expertise of our Shepherd. You must return to your Shepherd to have satisfying water. Follow after your Shepherd where even "in the wilderness shall waters break out, and streams in the desert. And the parched ground shall become a pool, and the thirsty land springs of water" (Isa. 35:6-7). Our Shepherd can provide under the most unlikely circumstances. "When the poor and needy seek water, and there is none, and their tongue faileth for thirst, I the LORD will hear them, I the God of Israel will not forsake them. I will open rivers in high places, and fountains in the midst of the valleys: I will make the wilderness a pool of water, and the dry land springs of water" (Isa. 41:17-18). Oh, for such a reviving of the water sources from our Shepherd!

Do not let the sorrows of your heart prove too overwhelming to deter you; no joys of this life are too captivating to detain you from your Shepherd. He is the fountain of life and He will make you "drink of the river of thy pleasures" (Ps. 36:8). "Drink" here means to drink abundantly or be soaked or drenched, yea, saturated with abundance. The word "pleasures" is the Hebrew word *edens* as pleasures provided by the Lord. Charles H. Spurgeon noted,

As they have the fruits of Eden to feed on, so shall they have the river of Paradise to drink from. God's everlasting love bears to us a constant and ample comfort, of which grace makes us to drink by faith, and then our pleasure is of the richest kind. The Lord not only brings us to this river, but makes us drink: herein we see the condescension of divine love. Heaven will, in the fullest sense, fulfil these words; but they who trust in the Lord enjoy the antepast even here. The happiness given to the faithful is that of God himself; purified spirits joy with the same joy as the Lord himself. 'That my joy may be in you, that your joy may be full.'

As previously intimated our Shepherd Jehovah-Jesus is the fountain, and He is of our nature or took our nature in order to open the fountain. "In that day there shall be a fountain opened to the house of David and to the inhabitants of Jerusalem for sin and for uncleanness" (Zech. 13:1). A fountain or spring shall be opened but not a cistern; here is a pool better than that of Siloam, which is by interpretation, *Sent*, John 9:7; here is a type of Christ, who "loved us, and washed us from our sins with his own blood, and hath made us kings and priests unto God and his Father; to him be glory and dominion for ever and ever. Amen," Rev 1:5, 6, [John Trapp].

As the Shepherd's sheep journey through this world they are all able to testify that they "have been all made to drink into one Spirit" (1 Cor. 12:13). The good or worthy Shepherd freely invites all the sheep of His flock to partake of these "still waters." Under the Old Testament era His voice was heard to say, "Ho, every one that thirsteth, come ye to the waters" (Isa. 55:1); and at the close of the New Testament era He closes with, "The Spirit and the bride say, come. And let him that heareth say, Come. And let him that is athirst come. And whosoever will, let him take the water of life freely" (Rev. 22:17). Our good Shepherd will gather His flock which He redeemed; for "the Lamb which is in the midst of the throne shall feed them, and shall lead them unto living fountains of waters" (Rev. 7:17). What glorious care!

There is a future prospect that the Shepherd has given His flock for He leads them to water—"And he shewed me a pure river of water of life, clear as crystal, proceeding out of the throne of God and of the Lamb" (Rev. 22:1). In the Garden in Eden, the first Paradise, connected with the first creation, we find a river — "a river went out of Eden to water the garden" (Gen. 2:10). When we come to Revelation 22:1 and the second Paradise, the new creation in Christ, we find another river, this river is not named but is called "a river of life." The earthly and the heavenly thus run parallel with each other, though the glory of the celestial is one, and the glory of the terrestrial is another.

Our Shepherd gives us many allusions to waters. "Thou shalt make them drink of the river of thy pleasures" (Ps. 36:8); "there is a river, the streams whereof shall make glad the city of God" (Ps. 46:4); "you enrich it with the river of God, which is full of water" (Ps. 65:9); "then had Thy peace been as a river" (Isa. 48:18); "the Lord shall be to us a place of broad rivers and streams" (Isa. 33:21).

The earthly streams by which our Shepherd leads us gives beauty, fertility, refreshment, life as well as satisfaction to the thirst. All these and much more the heavenly river does for us. In this river of life is the reality of those things of which the earthly river is the shadow. What would the first Adam's Paradise have been without the river? What would the second Adam's Paradise and city be without the river of life?

Take a while and contemplate this river of life which John described, and see its qualities and glories. It is a river of heaven. The last two chapters of Revelation speak of no earthly city, no earthly Paradise, no earthly tree of life, and no earthly river. It is a stream fed from heavenly sources, filled with heavenly water, and resplendent with heavenly beauty. Everything pertaining to its origin, and course, and nature, partakes of heaven. It is the river our Shepherd leads us by with its pure water and all that heaven contains of blessedness. Those who drink of it must drink immortality and love. "It is the river of God." To gaze on it, to wander by its banks, to bathe in its pure flood, to drink of its waters — this is heaven itself![*]

---

[*] See Appendix 3

CHAPTER 4
I Shall Not Want:
Because He Restores My Soul

I shall not want because He restores my soul. "He restoreth my soul" (v. 3a). There is no soul that goes lacking with this Shepherd. Spurgeon had a very succinct comment, "When the soul grows sorrowful he revives it; when it is sinful he sanctifies it; when it is weak he strengthens it. 'He' does it. His ministers could not do it if he did not. His Word would not avail by itself." Our worthy Shepherd restores our soul. He is the one to appeal to when we are low in grace! He is the One to revive us when we are spirituality drained. He is the One who controls the power in a thunder storm or hurricane, He can restore our weary souls. Go to Him who can restore the joy of your salvation to restore your soul.

We are informed from these words—"He restoreth my soul," that Jehovah-Jesus is the Restorer and that David was a wanderer who needed to be restored. The Psalmist does not try to conceal the truth of this but incorporates it as a part of his confession—"The LORD is my shepherd—He restoreth my soul." Remember the words by which David ended his longest Psalm; there he recites his experience—"I have gone astray like a lost sheep. Seek thy servant, for I do not forget thy commandments" (Ps. 119:176). How does a sheep get lost? It takes the safety of the shepherd and the fold for granted. It becomes wearied of the fold and longs for new pastures; yea, the grass on yonder hill is greener. It no longer follows the shepherd's footsteps. Though it hears the directions of the shepherd to the flock within it begins to refuse it. Bit by bit it starts drifting from the fold. The newly coveted pasture is sweet at first. The straying feet are tempted to go further. It at first has a sense of liberty and freedom. Then the shadows darken and evening captures it. Then it begins to sense possible trouble but morning light will remedy everything. Then the awareness of being alone arises. It begins to lose peace and a sense of safety. At first light it scurries to find a way back but cannot. Then thirst begins to hound it. Then the reality, it is lost!

For the Christian he likewise wanders away from the fold. He begins to neglect his praying. He no longer takes pleasure in the Bible. He no longer delights in fellowship. Private and then public worship are neglected. Fun and pleasures become dominant. The love and thankful attitude toward the Lord Jesus is forgotten. Sin no longer seems exceedingly sinful. The heart becomes more and more captured by the deceitfulness of sin and the feet begin to follow the well worn path of the worldly. Now you are lost or astray and need to be restored by your Shepherd (Luke 15:4-7).

When a sheep is lost it does not have any understanding about what direction to take. It ends up getting more lost than it was and thus further away from the fold. There is no sense of direction left, no sense of security left, no protection evident, no instinct for survival, no familiarity with the right way to go, etc. Consider being forlorn and melancholy as is the sheep that wandered so casually from the fold! The members of its flock, yea fellow companions are yet safe and happy, while the wanderer is lonely and miserable. The wandering sheep with wearied feet traverses the mountains, hill sides and empty valleys putting forth its pitiful bleating. Each step takes it further away from the fold and increases the dangers that are beginning to grow. The wanderer no longer has peace! Every direction it takes new troubles arise! No scenes that come before the eyes are familiar. There is not a recognizable sound or familiar bleat of a fellow sheep. Terror now glazes the darting eyes which become more frantic. The sheep wants to return to the fold. Every direction and exertion is expended to return to the familiar fold. It turns hither and thither but there is no recognizable trail back to the care of the shepherd. Over and over again the lonely wanderer expends its utmost energy only to fail. Barriers of briar and thorn are pressed through only to leave their prickly trophies. Bounding over all hostile terrain in a now frantic pace but home is not in sight. There is a sudden stop to catch breath and look around. Then there is a hopeful listening to sounds that begin to betray the ears with false interpretation. Away it goes in another direction but finally it sinks in weariness and panting upon the wayward track. There is alas no strength left and any enemy may easily overwhelm the wayward one. The darkness of the final night is rapidly falling, and its scent is caught by a ravenous wild beast which makes a triumphant howl. The helpless wanderer is now the prey to the destroyer! Suddenly! a friendly arm scoops it up. The shepherd had missed his lost sheep; he knew its danger was great and hastened to search for it; and now, at the last moment and with great joy he finds the hapless creature, lays it upon his shoulder and brings it back to the fold! What a vivid picture of being lost and then being found. One thinks of the gospel song, "There were ninety and nine that safely lay In the shelter of the fold, But one was out on the hills away, Far off from the gates of gold. Away on the mountains wild and bare, Away from the tender Shepherds care, Away from the tender Shepherd's Care." Consider the following elements:

First let us consider afresh who does the restoring. David, by the Holy Spirit's direction, uses the elegant picture of a shepherd's care of his sheep to reveal the love of God for His chosen people. "And ye my flock, the flock of my pasture, are men, and I am your God, saith the Lord GOD" (Ez. 34:31). "We are His people, and the sheep of His pasture" (Ps. 100:3). "He is our God: and we are the people of his pasture, and the sheep of his hand" (Ps. 95:7). It is the worthy Shepherd who is none other than our Lord Jesus Christ. He is Jehovah and the Shepherd promised: "Give ear, O Shepherd of Israel, thou that leadest Joseph like a flock; thou that dwellest between the cherubim, shine forth.... Turn us again, O God, and cause thy face to shine; and we shall be saved" (Ps. 80:1, 3). "He shall feed his flock like a shepherd: he shall gather the lambs with his arm, and carry them in his bosom, and shall gently lead those that are with young" (Isa. 40:11). The Shepherd's sacrifice was predicted. "Awake, O sword, against my shepherd, and against the man that is my fellow, saith the LORD of hosts: smite the shepherd, and the sheep shall be scattered: and I will turn mine hand upon the little ones" (Zech. 13:7). Jesus owned the relation and confirmed the prophecy when He said, "I lay down my life for the sheep" (John 10:15). He verified the value of His sacrifice for the sheep when He rose again the third day from the dead (1 Cor. 15:4). He was "declared to be the Son of God with power, according to the spirit of holiness, by the resurrection from the dead" (Rom. 1:4). He was declared to be the "great Shepherd of the sheep" who is "the Shepherd and Bishop of our souls." There is little advantage for a person who has not individually received "the redemption that is in Christ Jesus." Then you could not say, "The LORD is *my* shepherd." My friend if you have no Saviour you have no Shepherd. You need to come to Christ in repentance of sin and faith in Jesus.

Second, the Shepherd "restoreth my soul." What is the meaning of the term "restore?" The sense of "restore" in this text takes into consideration that the way of righteousness has been forsaken; then by the Shepherd's initiative the straying sheep has been restored or returned to the former condition. Consider Isaiah, "And they that shall be of thee shall build the old waste places: thou shalt raise up the foundations of many generations; and thou shalt be called, The repairer of the breach, The restorer of paths to dwell in" (Isa. 58:12). Our Shepherd is "the restorer of paths to dwell in" for the way had been temporarily abandoned but He brings back or brings them again to the way of righteousness and away from the way that seems right unto men, which is the way of death. Jeremiah used this word "restore" when quoting Jehovah of hosts who said, "I will bring Israel again to his habitation" (Jer. 50:19). This word is also compatible with the nature of sheep that are so prone to wander off and need to be restored to the fold. Consider Jehovah's depiction of His children, "The LORD hath spoken, I have nourished and brought up children, and they have rebelled against me. The ox knoweth his owner and the ass his master's crib: but Israel doth not know, my people doth not consider. Ah sinful nation, a people laden with iniquity, a seed of evildoers, children that are corrupters: they have forsaken the LORD, they have provoked the Holy One of Israel unto anger, they are gone away backward" (Isa. 1:2-4). Only Jehovah-Jesus can restore! Thank God He restores the backslider.

Third, there is the restoration of the sheep by the Shepherd. Here we consider the pastoral office of Christ who provides for His sheep, who gives direction for His sheep and who makes a defense for His sheep. [1] The worthy Shepherd provides for His sheep. We saw this in verse 2 where He makes them lie down in green pastures and He leads them beside still waters. [2] The worthy Shepherd is vigilant toward His sheep by superintending their steps. He "restores" and "leads" them.

There is a twofold aspect to "He restoreth my soul." Our Shepherd by grace recovers His wayward sheep and directs the renewal of their obedience. Sheep are so prone to wander that it has become a proverb. The further a sheep strays the more bewildered he becomes and the further he will stray. Thus the picture is of a Christian, though renewed in the spirit of the mind carries with him the tendency of straying (Eph. 4:23). Yes, the remnant of corruption remains in departing from the living God. Just think about what would happen if the influence of our Shepherd were removed from the most enlightened and tested sheep; that sheep would immediately go astray. We must be kept by the power of God.

Think of the examples of men our Lord gives us in His Word; they are not obscure or dubious professors of faith, but men of eminent faith and greatly favored of God. Peter is an example, he denied the Lord Christ. Or we could contemplate David taking advantage of Bathsheba ending in the death of her husband and the death of the child born to her and David. Think of the impact this had for the sword did not depart from his house (2 Sam. 11 & 12) and he lost the joy of his salvation (Ps. 51). One writer asked:

How far [can] the regenerate go, it is not for us to conjecture, and it would be madness to try. That they shall not finally perish, is one of the plainest promises of the Bible. But between the circumspection of grace and the damnation of hell, there is ample room for sinning and for chastisement. To lose your comfort it is not necessary that you lose your soul. Even within the boundaries of pardon, there are a thousand deviations from duty sufficient to mar your peace, and bring you under the rod. No inconsistency can be traced between the Lord's *forgiving his people*, and his *taking vengeance of their inventions*. How many afflicted have borne witness to these truths! How do our own hearts smite us for our aberrations from the *straight path* of God's commandments! And how sad is the condition of those who, duped by the *deceitfulness of sin,* have *left their first love*, and gone away after vanity! Lost attainment, forfeited joy, withering graces, barrenness, leanness, lameness, and a long train of kindred miseries, follow the steps of disobedience. If the *end* be not *destruction*, it is because *the issues from death belong unto the Lord our God.* [John M. Mason]

The worthy Shepherd's eye is habitually upon the way of the wandering sheep, and at the most critical moment when their destruction seems to be imminent He steps in and takes them into His arms and carries them back to His pasture and fold (Isa. 40:10-11). The way the Shepherd injects Himself into the retrieval situation is noteworthy.

[a] The Shepherd comes unawares and with surprise. The wayward sheep is in such a backslidden condition that the Lord is far from his thoughts. To the conscience suddenly the Lord speaks with a voice that recalls to the memory numerous mercies and awakens from the slumber. The eyes open and the dream is at an end! They stand amazed in the presence of their Shepherd Jehovah-Jesus; astounded they are unable to escape. Like the cry, "What doest thou here, Elijah" (1 Kings 19:9, 13)?

Charles H. Spurgeon as a boy lived with his grandparents. His grandfather was a pastor. He ministered to the Stambourne "Meeting House." Young Charles had evidently heard some discussion regarding Thomas Roads an unruly church member. Roads had been regularly frequenting a public-house to the grief of his godly pastor. Little Charles one day exclaimed in his grandfather's hearing, "I'll kill old Roads, that I will!" The elderly minister said, "Hush, hush! My dear, you mustn't talk so; it's very wrong, you know, and you'll get taken up by the police, if you do anything wrong." "I shall not do anything bad; but I'll kill him though, that I will." The boy Spurgeon left his grandfather in contemplation. Sometime later the boy came in declaring, "I've killed old Roads; he'll never grieve my dear grandpa any more." Grandfather Spurgeon said, "My dear child, what have you done? Where have you been?" He rejoined, "I haven't been doing any harm, grandpa. I've been about the Lord's work, that's all." That was all they could get out of young Charles. Soon the mystery was cleared up. "Old Roads" called to see his pastor, and, with downcast looks and evident sorrow of heart, narrated the story of how he had been killed, somewhat in this fashion: "I'm very sorry indeed, my dear pastor, to have caused you such grief and trouble. It was very wrong, I know; but I always loved you, and wouldn't have done it if I'd only thought." With encouragement he went on, "I was a-sitting in the public just having my pipe and mug of beer, when that child comes in—to think an old man like me should be took to task, and reproved by a bit of a child like that! Well, he points at me with his finger, just so, and says, 'What doest thou here, Elijah? Sitting with the ungodly; and you a member of a church, and breaking your pastor's heart. I'm ashamed of you! I wouldn't break my pastor's heart, I'm sure.' And then he walks away. Well, I did feel angry, but I knew it was all true, and I was guilty...." Roads hurried to a private place and cast himself before the Lord calling for mercy and asking for forgiveness.

[b] The Shepherd communes with His sheep about the nature and humiliation of sin. The wayward sheep's accusers rise up in the form of the Shepherd's former kindnesses, His forgotten love, His injured sacrifice, His grieved Spirit, His impugned promises, etc. The sheep is seized with amazement, the bitterness of self-reproach, the depth of self-abhorrence. The sheep moans in Ezra's words, "O my God, I am ashamed, and blush to lift up my face to thee, my God: for our iniquities are increased over our head, and our trespass is grown up unto the heavens" (Ezra 9:6). It is a sad state to be a prodigal from the Shepherd. "Hast thou not procured this unto thyself, in that thou hast forsaken the LORD thy God, when he led thee by the way? ... Thine own wickedness shall correct [chastise] thee, and thy backslidings shall reprove [severely rebuke] thee: know therefore and see that it is an evil thing and bitter, that thou

hast forsaken the LORD thy God, and that my fear is not in thee, saith the Lord GOD of hosts" (Jer. 2:17, 19). The stray sheep will be visited with remorse and compunction belonging to the discipline of the Father's house: for He has said, that "If his children forsake my law, and walk not in my judgments; If they break my statutes, and keep not my commandments; then will I visit their transgression with the rod, and their iniquity with stripes. Nevertheless my lovingkindness will I not utterly take from him, nor suffer my faithfulness to fail" (Ps. 89:30-33). Here again is the language of the shepherd. Clearly his chastening though painful is merciful so that the sheep "be not condemned with the world." Our all-wise Shepherd can reign in our waywardness. When they have run their providential course and the purity of the gospel is vindicated by the sheep's sweets of sin are turned into wormwood and gall. Once again the "beauty of holiness" is visible and the way is prepared for the binding up of the broken heart.

[c] The worthy Shepherd restores peace to His mourning sheep. Like David there is the cry for mercy, the blotting out of sin, cleansing and restoration (Ps. 51:12). These are led to renounce their waywardness and confess their sins for Jesus Christ's blood cleanses from all sin and if we confess our sins He is faithful and just to forgive us our sins, and to cleanse us from all unrighteousness (1 John 1:7, 9). Oh, the patience of our Shepherd to retrieve His sheep from being astray. His compassion, forgiveness and care are evident. "Thou shalt know that I am the LORD: That thou mayest remember, and be confounded, and never open thy mouth any more because of thy shame, when I am pacified toward thee for all that thou hast done, saith the Lord GOD" (Ez. 16:62-63). The Shepherd opens the springs

of contrition. "Rivers of waters run down mine eyes" (Ps. 119:136) as the sheep abandons his waywardness. Once the Shepherd begins His restoration the sheep say, "I thought on my ways (manner of conduct), and turned my feet unto thy testimonies" (Ps. 119:59). Here is a repentant sheep. The return is to the Shepherd and Bishop of our souls by which they regain fellowship with Him. Now they crucify the flesh with the affections and lusts. Return to Jehovah and say, "Take away all iniquity, and receive us graciously" (Hosea 14:1-2). The Shepherd has healed their straying. "I will heal their backsliding [the wound of their waywardness], I will love them freely: for mine anger is turned away from him. I will be as the dew unto Israel [God's grace is like the dew]: he shall grow as the lily, and cast forth his roots as Lebanon. His branches shall spread, and his beauty shall be as the olive tree, and his smell as Lebanon. They that dwell under his shadow shall return; they shall revive as the corn, and grow as the vine" (Hosea 14:4-7).

CONCLUSION: Christ restores His people His own way and on His own schedule. The process of restoring the soul includes,

[1] A conviction of sin and folly in straying from the Lord.

[2] A heartfelt self-reproach and sorrow over sinning against God.

[3] A fear of having displeased the Lord and a deserving of His judgment.

[4] A soul distress over a sense of the evil of sin.

[5]A longing to be restored to fellowship with God

The Psalmist wrote, "I have gone astray like a lost sheep. Seek thy servant, for I do not forget thy commandments" (Ps. 119:176). Here is a confession of having gone astray and a plea for the Shepherd to seek His servant.

CHAPTER 5
I Shall Not Want:
Because He Leads Me in the Paths of Righteousness

I shall not want because He leads me in the paths of righteousness for His name's sake. The sheep can say, "He leadeth me in the paths of righteousness for his name's sake" (v. 3b). The Shepherd also "leadeth me beside the still waters." Most of us have taken a path. I remember the path through the field from the house where I grew up to my aunt and uncle's house. That path was through a hay field but was so well trodden that it never grew over.

In this portion of verse 3 we are reminded: [1] David identifies what the Shepherd does—"He leadeth me," [2] David identifies where the Shepherd leads—"in the paths of righteousness," and [3] David reveals why the Shepherd leads—"for his name's sake."

First, **David identifies what the Shepherd does—** "He leadeth me." This is not the first mention of His leading as briefly noted and recorded by Holy Spirit inspiration, "He leadeth me beside the still waters." Now we see His leadership again. This reinforces the fact that one of the primary activities of a shepherd is the leading of sheep. In David's part of the world sheep were "led" and not driven. This is the way David handled sheep, he led them. The

Hebrew word "lead" indicates that it is done with a gentle and gradual leading. When the sheep hear the voice of their shepherd there is a reaction; John wrote of Jesus' shepherding which is the same, "and he calleth his own sheep by name, and *leadeth them out*. And when he putteth forth his own sheep, *he goeth before them*, and the sheep follow him: for they know his voice" (John 10:3-4). Here is the reason they follow His leading: they know him and his voice. The sheep trust the shepherd's leading for his leadership is and has been for their good. David and our Shepherd "always" leads us for our good for He makes all things work together for our good (Rom. 8:28).

Between the first "leading" and the second there is the restoring of the soul (vv. 2-3). Surely the leading coming on the heels of this restoration to the fold fosters the increase in the desire to properly follow the Shepherd. The faithfulness of the Shepherd's rescue shows the quality of His shepherding. So when He calls them by name and leads them out; they are even more diligent to stay close to His footsteps; and the paths He chooses for them even though it may be rough, steep, narrow and dangerous are under the shepherd's direction. He knows what is best for them and they can trust Him. This is the conclusion of every restored sheep in the flock of Christ. They have been restored to peace, joy, purity, happiness and holiness. This is what David had desired—"Restore unto me the joy of thy salvation; and uphold me with thy free spirit" (Ps. 51:12). This prayer of David was answered as we saw in the last message—"He restoreth my soul."

What a great boon it is to know that the Shepherd leads you. David could attest to the blessing of this personally when he wrote, "He leadeth *me*." He had experienced the leading by still waters, he had been reclaimed from wandering and now to be led in the glorious paths of righteousness. The Shepherd of the spiritual flock first calls His sheep effectually by the Spirit to Himself in salvation from the world. Then He keeps them even in their times of wandering causing them to persevere. The path of obedience is where they are ever returned in this life by the Shepherd. They are "kept by the power of God through faith unto salvation ready to be revealed in the last time" (1 Pet. 1:5). The heavenward steps of the sheep are under the leadership of the Shepherd. Therefore, how can the sheep prone to wander be kept on the proper path? and sealed unto the day of redemption. The hymn "Come thou Fount" by Robert Robinson clearly identifies the issue [stanza 3]:

> O to grace how great a debtor
> Daily I'm constrained to be;
> Let that grace now, like a fetter,
> Bind my wand'ring heart to thee.
> Prone to wander, Lord, I feel it,
> Prone to leave the God I love;
> Here's my heart, O take and seal it,
> Seal it for thy courts above.

Even after the believer has wandered; even after he has bitterly felt the sinfulness of his straying from the Lord; even then he cannot be trusted to act as his own guide. Jeremiah confessed, "O LORD, I know that the way of man is not in himself: it is not in man that walketh to direct his steps" (Jer. 10:23). The Lord's sheep in this world cannot walk by themselves; they are not trustworthy for they always need the Shepherd. The Shepherd must choose the path, direct the steps, order the events, form the plan, regulate the desire and go before the sheep. David understood this by God's grace and often wrote of it. Though he had enjoyed the Shepherd's abundance, experienced His protection and known His guidance he realized his daily need of Him. David could say, "I recline amid green pastures, but it is *my Shepherd* who makes me to lie down! I drink from still waters because *my Shepherd* leads me continually. I am brought back from my wanderings by His care for His mercy alone restores my soul! And I am now walking in the paths of righteousness because *my Shepherd* condescends to lead me for His name's sake!"

Years ago there was an English guide in the Holy Land and he was leading a party of tourists. He had explained to them about the shepherds and how they always led their sheep. On their tour one day a member of the party called the attention of their guide to the fact that there was a man driving a flock of sheep. "I thought you said shepherds never drove their sheep." The instant reply was "Yes, that is true." As the scene was pointed out to him he declared that he would check into the situation. So the guide crossed into the area where the man was busy driving sheep. "Excuse me, Mr. Shepherd, why are you driving your sheep? I thought that was never done?" The man looked at him a bit bewildered and said, "Shepherd? I'm not a shepherd—I'm a butcher."

Our Shepherd controls all events and thus has the power to use special providence to lead His sheep. Earthly history is so appointed and designed by our great heavenly Shepherd to lead us in the proper paths. What is providential for us? Our family, time and place of birth, our place in society, our amount of education, our relatives and friends, our business and calling in life, our successes and reverses, our joys and sorrows, our health or sickness, our strength or weakness, our wealth or poverty are all within His providential means in leading His sheep. The flock is led by outward dispensations of providence and by inward works of His Spirit.

Our Shepherd leads by His Spirit who works in our minds and hearts. "As many as are led by the Spirit of God, they are the sons of God" (Rom. 8:14). The awakening of emotions, the production of impressions, the enlightening of conscience, the opening of the Word of God to the understanding, the warnings that are given, the promises that are made, and these all by the work of the Holy Spirit. Remember when Paul and Barnabas were "forbidden of the Holy Ghost to preach the word in Asia, After they were come to Mysia, they assayed to go into Bithynia: but the Spirit suffered them not" (Acts 16:6-7, see vv. 9-10). The Spirit of God leads us in prayer, praise, worship and the drawing out of our affections. When tempted to stray He leads us to go right. The Holy Spirit whispers within us, "This is the way: walk ye in it." The Spirit not only directs and encourages but persuades and convicts our hearts to be loyal to our Shepherd. He teaches us to say, "I will run the way of thy commandments, when thou shalt enlarge my heart" (Ps. 119:32).

David's words, "He leadeth me" implies not just the guidance of the Shepherd but the obedience in the following by the sheep. All His flock is made willing to be led. The drawing of God the Father through the love of the Lord Jesus and by the power of the Holy Spirit is manifest in this leading. Yes, "The love of Christ constraineth us" (2 Cor. 5:14). The Holy Spirit works to wean us from the world, to sanctify our affections, to subdue our wills that we might be obedient and faithful to our Shepherd. The prophet Ezekiel said, "A new heart also will I give you, and a new spirit will I put within you: and I will take away the stony heart out of your flesh, and I will give you an heart of flesh. And I will put my spirit within you, and cause you to walk in my statutes, and ye shall keep my judgments, and do them" (Ez. 36:26-27). The Holy Spirit directs us to enter into His paths, to walk those paths and to persevere in those paths to the end. He causes us in times of need to be "looking unto Jesus the author and finisher of our faith; who for the joy that was set before him endured the cross, despising the shame, and is set down at the right hand of the throne of God" (Heb. 12:2). When sheep follow their Shepherd, they are always in the right path, always safe, always supplied, always able to worship. If the sheep stay under the pillar of fire by night they have light and are kept warm. If the sheep stay under the cloud by day they are protected from damaging heat and have light. Both those provisions preclude wandering.

Second, David identifies where the Shepherd leads—"in the paths of righteousness." The word "righteousness" in the original means the right thing morally or legally, and rectitude in the ethical sense as what ought to be (Ps. 15:2; Isa. 64:5). Its essential meaning reveals an unswerving adherence to the standard or rule set down by God. Righteous conduct issues from a new heart as we saw in Ezekiel (Ez. 36:25-27) and one who has this attribute will live his daily life by the principle of right (Hab. 2:4). "This quality indeed may be viewed, according to Scripture, in two lights. In its relative aspect it implies conformity with the line or rule of God's law; in its absolute aspect it is the exhibition of love to God and to one's neighbor, because love is the fulfilling of the law" [Robert B. Girdlestone, *Synonyms of the Old Testament*].

Transferred to moral subjects, this figurative language marks the distinction between good and bad, whether in doctrine or practice. Accordingly we consider the law of God as the *rule* or *standard* to which every principle and action must be referred. All its precepts are *righteous*; conformity with them is *righteousness*; and, consequently, *paths of righteousness* signify that habitual and actual holiness which they prescribe both for the heart and life. But, then, we must remember that the divine law as regulating *Christian* obedience is, in a very peculiar sense, the law of Christ. For, as the representative of His people, He has, on the one hand, divested it of its covenant-form by fulfilling its injunctions in the righteousness of His life, and extinguishing its penalty in the sacrifice of His death, so that it neither justifies nor condemns them. And on the other, He has given them, as the test and measure of their sanctification, this very law, to keep which they are both required by His authority, and constrained by His love. Thus connected, its precepts ascertain and promote evangelical purity, and are transcendently *paths of righteousness* [Mason].

The sheep has the law as a set of guard rails to keep him within the scope of the path. "And an highway shall be there, and a way, and it shall be called The way of holiness; the unclean shall not pass over it; but it shall be for those: the wayfaring men, though fools, shall not err therein" (Isa. 35:8). The basis of our righteousness toward God and man is important—"I lead in the way of righteousness, in the midst of the paths of judgment: that I may cause those that love me to inherit substance; and I will fill their treasures" (Prov. 8:20-21). The basis of God's dwelling place— "Righteousness and judgment are the habitation (or foundation) of God's throne" (Ps. 97:2). The paths of righteousness are to lead to the presence of God. Our Shepherd is Himself the greatest example of walking in the paths of righteousness. Our Lord Jesus' by every action in life was distinguished by pure and perfect righteousness.

He has not left a thorn in our path which did not pierce His own blessed foot: not one, of which His blood will not counteract the poison, and heal the wound—That in all the opposition which His people have to encounter, He is the first to perceive the foe, and to sustain the onset; for *their King shall pass before them, and the Lord on the head of them*—that he *enlarges their hearts to run the way of His commandments*: His love *constraining* them, both as a motive and a principle, to *live not unto themselves, but unto him that died for them and rose again*; a constraint which liberates their will, so that they *walk at liberty,* and without which they would infallibly revert back into bondage. Summarily, they know nothing, perform nothing, and are nothing, but in their Leader's might. He is the *Lord their strength, who guides them with his counsel,* as a pledge that He will *afterward receive them to glory* [Mason].

The path of the sheep should, as a norm, be righteous— "Whosoever is born of God doth not commit [or habitually practice] sin; for his seed remaineth in him: and he cannot [habitually practice] sin, because he is born of God. In this the children of God are manifest, and the children of the devil: whosoever doeth not righteousness is not of God, neither he that loveth not his brother" (1 John 3:9-10). We are deceiving ourselves to claim the name "Christian" unless we endeavor to bridle our tongue, curb our temper, restrain our envy, seek to control our uncharitable and covetous thoughts and mortify sinful lusts and appetites. Our Shepherd declared, "And whosoever doth not bear his cross, and come after me, cannot be my disciple" (Luke 14:27). The very name of our Saviour declares, "He shall save his people from their sins" (Matt. 1:21). How does Jesus bless you? "Unto you first God, having raised up his Son Jesus, sent him to bless you, in turning away every one of you from his iniquities" (Acts 3:26).

The sheep are concerned to be in the path of righteousness. This leads them to pray to that end. David prayed, "Hold up my goings in thy paths, that my footsteps slip not. I have called upon thee, for thou wilt hear me, O God: incline thine ear unto me, and hear my speech" (Ps. 17:5-6). He also prayed, "Cause me to know the way wherein I should walk; for I lift up my soul unto thee.... Thou art my God: thy spirit is good; lead me into the land of uprightness" (Ps. 143:8, 10). Also he prayed, "Teach me thy way, O LORD, and lead me in a plain path, because of mine enemies" (Ps. 27:11). Oh, that glorious plea, "Search me, O God, and know my heart: try me, and know my thoughts: And see if there be any wicked way in me, and lead me in the way everlasting" (Ps. 139:23-24).

Third, David revealed why the Shepherd leads— "for his name's sake." The name of Jesus, who is our Shepherd, includes all the excellencies of his person, offices and work. His purpose in the incarnation in human flesh, in His impeccable life, in His sacrificial death, in His victorious resurrection and in His heavenly rule was for His Father's glory and the redemption of His sheep. His name is displayed in the redemption of His sheep. His name was displayed in the glorification of His sheep. He is the author and finisher of our faith, because of the joy that was set before Him He endured the cross, despising the same and was seated at the right hand of the throne of God (Heb. 12:2). He was highly exalted and given a name above every name *that at His name every knee should bow and every tongue confess* His Lordship (Phil. 2:9-11).

His name is at stake regarding His faithfulness in leading His sheep. If He were to fail in His sheep's preservation it would tarnish His name. If they were to go astray into final apostasy His name would be dishonored. And His promise would be broken that not one of them can be lost without the ruin of His name (John 17:12). "For the LORD will not forsake his people for *his great name's sake*: because it hath pleased the Lord to make you his people" (1 Sam. 12:22).

John Stevenson wrote,

When therefore the Psalmist says, 'He leadeth men in the paths of righteousness for his name's sake,' we are to understand him to signify, in the *first place*, that the Lord was pleased so to do of His own mercy and grace, and for the manifestation of his own love and power and glory! We understand him, in the *second place*, to affirm that, after he had gone astray, it was not on account of any value or excellency which he possessed that fresh kindness had been exhibited towards him, but that the Lord had restored him to the fold, and was now leading him in the paths of righteousness for the glory of his own name!

Consider the inspired words in Isaiah, "For my name's sake will I defer mine anger.... For mine own sake, even for mine own sake, will I do it: for how should *my name* be polluted? and I will not give my glory unto another" (Isa. 48:9, 11). Mercy saves and mercy keeps.

For His name sake He leads His sheep in paths of righteousness and insures their acceptance before the throne of grace. A wayward sheep might be disconsolate and say "He might overlook me" but would it be true that He would overlook a sheep? No! He cannot "for his name's sake." No one can charge our Shepherd with being indifferent toward His name or those He promised not to lose. His name is as good as possessing His eternal salvation. Yes, "him that cometh to me I will in no wise cast out." Remember David's declaration and prayer, "All the paths of the LORD are mercy and truth unto such as keep his covenant and his testimonies. For *thy name's sake*, O LORD, pardon mine iniquity; for it is great" (Ps. 25:10-11). Remember David's prayer, ""Quicken me, O LORD, for *thy name's sake*: for thy righteousness' sake bring my soul out of trouble" (Ps. 143:11). Our Shepherd will honor His "great name." "There is none like unto thee, O LORD; thou art great, and *thy name* is great in might" (Jer. 10:6). Jeremiah's plea was, "Do not abhor us, for *thy name's sake*, do not disgrace the throne of thy glory: remember, break not thy covenant with us" (Jer. 14:21). His name's sake is why He will not abhor or disgrace or break His part of the covenant. We are to preach that there is none other name under heaven given among men whereby we must be saved (Acts 4:12), we should preach boldly in Jesus' name (Acts

9:27), men are to believe on His name (1 John 3:23; 5:13), and at Jesus' name every knee will bow (Phil. 2:10). His is a powerful name!

His name gives us a passage to prayer. Our Shepherd Jehovah-Jesus gave His sheep this assurance, "Whatsoever ye shall ask the Father *in my name*, he will give it you" (John 16:23). "If ye shall ask any thing *in my name*, I will do it" (John 14:14). How did the sheep pray in David's time? "For *thy name's sake*, O LORD, pardon mine iniquity; for it is great" (Ps. 25:11). "Help us, O God of our salvation, for the glory of *thy name*: and deliver us, and purge away our sins, for *thy name's sake*" (Ps. 79:9). Daniel was also a man of prayer. How did he pray? "O Lord, hear; O Lord, forgive; O Lord, hearken and do; defer not, for thine own sake, O my God: for thy city and thy people are called by *thy name*" (Dan. 9:19).

Our Shepherd's name is a focal point for His sheep. We may rejoice in His name (Ps. 89:16). His name is an object of boasting in the Lord (Ps. 34:2). His name is above every name.

CONCLUSION: Consider the promises of our Shepherd as Isaiah recorded, "And I will bring the blind by a way that they knew not; I will lead them in paths that they have not known: I will make darkness light before them, and crooked things straight. These things will I do unto them, and not forsake them" (Isa. 42:16). How glorious!

The Lord's sheep have been justified by faith and have the imputed righteousness of Christ."The path of the just is as the shining light, that shinneth more and more unto the perfect day" (Prov. 4:18). We eventually enter the land of celestial light. Not only does Jehovah-Jesus lead us by a righteous path but He provides His righteousness to make us acceptable and He has prepared a place for us. Yes, we are accepted in the Beloved. "In the way of righteousness is life; and in the pathway thereof there is not death" (Prov. 12:28). Just think we have an ever-living Shepherd with a never-dying flock. He leads us in "the way everlasting." Because He lives we shall live also. Our eternity is resting in Him. The Lord our Shepherd and He is the Lord our righteousness. The *Trinity Hymnal* #415 has

1. God, be merciful to me;
   On Thy grace I rest my plea
   Plenteous in compassion Thou,
   Blot out my transgressions now;
   Wash me, make me pure within;
   Cleanse, O cleanse me from my sin.

2. My transgressions I confess;
   Grief and guilt my soul oppress.
   I have sinned against Thy grace,
   And provoked Thee to Thy face.
   I confess Thy judgment just;
   Speechless, I Thy mercy trust.

3. I am evil, born in sin;
   Thou desirest truth within.
   Thou alone my Savior art,
   Teach Thy wisdom to my heart;
   Make me pure, Thy grace bestow,
   Wash me whiter than the snow.

4. Broken, humbled to the dust
   By Thy wrath and judgment just,
   Let my contrite heart rejoice,
   And in gladness hear Thy voice;
   From my sins O hide Thy face,
   Blot them out in boundless grace.

5. Gracious God, my heart renew,
   Make my spirit right and true.
   Cast me not away from Thee,
   Let Thy Spirit dwell in me;

Thy salvation's joy impart,
Steadfast make my willing heart.

6. Sinners then shall learn from me,
And return, O God, to Thee
Savior all my guilt remove,
And my tongue shall sing Thy love
Touch my silent lips, O Lord,
And my mouth shall praise accord.

From *The Scottish Psalter*

Do you delight to follow your Shepherd? Do you delight to worship this One who makes provision for you terrestrially and eternally? Have you come into His courts with praise and thanksgiving? Yes, He leads me in the paths of righteousness for His name's sake.

John Calvin was right, "Certainly His choosing us to be His sheep, proceeds entirely from His free and sovereign goodness."

Section 2

David Confessed: Jehovah-Jesus Is My Shepherd Therefore I Will Fear No Evil

CHAPTER 6
I Will Fear No Evil:
What Does That Mean?

Psalm 23 is David's "Confession." *First,* David confessed: Jehovah-Jesus is My Shepherd therefore I shall not want (vv. 1-3). *Second,* David confessed: Jehovah-Jesus is My Shepherd therefore I will fear no evil (vv. 4-5). *Third,* David confessed: Jehovah-Jesus is My Shepherd therefore I shall dwell in the house forever (v. 6).

What our Shepherd does for us translates into the greatest care in time and for eternity. Consider how verses 4 and 5 break down: First, What does that mean—I will fear no evil? Second, Where do we not fear evil—walking through the valley of the shadow of death? Third, Why do we not need to fear evil—our Shepherd intervenes: [1] "For Thou art with me;" [2] "Thy rod and Thy staff they comfort me;" [3] "Thou preparest a table before me in the presence of mine enemies;" [4] "Thou anointest [a] my head with oil, [b] my cup runs over."

What does that mean—I will fear no evil? Remember there are three things that David declares as a result of Jehovah-Jesus being his Shepherd: [1] I shall not want, [2] I will fear no evil, and [3] I will dwell in the house of Jehovah forever. We come to the second result of Jehovah being his Shepherd—"I will fear no evil." Primarily in Psalm 23 we are reminded that while walking through the valley of the shadow of death David declares that this experience was without fear of a malicious result because the Shepherd was accompanying him. Yes, remember "The LORD is my shepherd," says David.

James Janeway (1636-1674), a Puritan, was a remarkable man of piety, writing, and devotion to the Lord. The Act of Uniformity in England cut him off from the house of God and separated him from those he pastored. During the plague he was assiduous in visiting the sick, being singularly preserved from the plague. At first he preached in empty church buildings. Then he collected a congregation at Rotherhithe, where he was greatly used and after the plague the church grew. While he was walking along Rotherhithe Wall one day he was shot at but the bullet only went through his hat. This exasperated the enemies of Christ and they began to make more attempts on his life, but the Lord preserved him. On one occasion soldiers broke into the meeting house and would have taken him out of the pulpit when the bench on which they stood broke and in the confusion he escaped. Another attempt was made to seize him when he was preaching at the home of a gardener but he threw himself on the ground, and his friends covered him with cabbage leaves. In God's time he died, he was thirty-eight. During his last illness he had some bouts of melancholy, but it pleased God to banish them and not long before his death he said death was easy as he shut his eyes, saying, "Here am I longing to be silent in the dust, and to enjoy Christ in glory."

In the light of who his Shepherd was David declared, "I will fear no evil." However, at this point perhaps it would be good to deal with "fear" in a broader sense. Definitively the "fear" mentioned in God's Word is a twofold kind of fear: [1] there is the emotional and intellectual anticipation of harm; and [2] there is the positive feeling of awe or reverence of God which is expressed in holy living or worship. Of this second definition Webster said, "The *fear* of God is a holy awe or reverence of God and his laws, which springs from a just view and real love of the divine character, leading the subjects of it to hate and shun every thing that can offend such a holy being, and inclining them to aim at perfect obedience. This is *filial* fear." Of the first definition Webster said there is "*Slavish* fear (which is) the effect or consequence of guilt; it is the painful apprehension of merited punishment. Rom. 8." The word "evil" means a malignant, noxious, injurious, hurtful, painful, hideous, fierce encounter. As a result of man's fall in Adam there is an innate fear of events and the future.

Man as a result of sinning against the holy God has innate fears of the repercussions of his actions unless his conscience is seared (1 Tim. 4:2). The origin of fear and death were at the fall of man in Adam (Gen. 2:7, 17; 3:6, 9 ff., 15, 17, 24). In Genesis 3 we learn of human fears in their inception. *Fear* was first marked by God's displeasure and then by fear of His judgment (Gen. 3:10). Adam and Eve hid themselves from the Saviour-God's presence (Jehovah) as a first sign of the impact of sin (Gen. 3:8). Remember what Adam said, "I heard Thy voice in the garden, and I was afraid, because I was naked; and I hid myself" (Gen. 3:10). There was a sense of present death ("thou shalt surely die") and also the fear of future death. They literally died the day they ate the forbidden fruit, their hearts established their condemnation and fear became a reality. There was real shame because of nakedness and real fear of physical death. Guilt was the real cause of their fear for they were spiritually doomed as under the curse. Their shame and fear resulted in their hiding from God so as not to encounter Him for "the carnal mind is enmity against God" (Rom. 8:7). Although God knew where they were He calls out "Where art thou" (Gen. 3:9). The reply, as we noted was, "I was afraid." This led Jehovah God's inquiry as to the cause (Gen. 3:11 ff.). Donald MacDonald in his superb *The Biblical Doctrine of Creation and the Fall* wrote,

This fear, then, did not originate from any tempest in the world without; it is not occasioned by any dark clouds or portents in the skies above, or any quaking of the earth under foot: ... at the time when the Almighty and Beneficent Creator visited His subjects, and asked the man formed in His image, 'Where art thou?' and yet the fear was not imaginary; it was real and well grounded, and the more so that it sprung from something appertaining to the man himself, something personal, from which he could not escape or shake himself free.... But although the fear was by Adam himself ascribed to a personal but bodily defect of which he had become conscious, it was nothing other than the feeling of guilt and consequent exposure, helpless and naked, to Divine wrath; and, in whatever way he might try to hide the matter from God or from himself, conscience would not fail to connect it with the act of disobedience."

Man as a result of the fall became a fear collector for he had the fear of God, the fear of death, the fear of fellow-man, the fear of beasts, the fear of hunger, etc. Only a saving relationship with the Lord through the redemptive work of Christ can remove the fear. "The wicked flee when no man pursueth" (Prov. 28:1). Their consciences began to terrorize them and make them feel vulnerable and afraid. The Emperor Domitian, one of the vilest wretches that ever disgraced humanity, who made it his boast that he had steeled his face against a blush; this same wretch because of a fear of assassination caused the ends of the corridor in which he took exercise to be lined with polished marble, to reflect the image of any one behind him. Cain feared because he was an outlaw under the curse of God; he believed everyone was out to kill him (Gen. 4:12-14). "Such were those cursed Canaanites that were chased by God's hornets sent among them" as one has said "that is, by the blood hounds of their own consciences (Joshua 24:12). Such were those Syrians that, struck with a panic terror, fled for their lives, and left their rich camp for a booty to the Israelites (2 Kings 7:7).... As the Spanish fleet, in 1588, *Venit, vidit, fugit,* (he came, he saw, he fled) as the Zealanders thereupon stamped their new coin" thus remarked John Trapp. The Dutch also stamped new monies with this invincible motto, *Impius fugit, nemine sequente,* "The wicked fly when no man pursueth" in quoting Proverbs 28:1. Have you ever heard, "He is frightened of his own shadow." This kind of fear was expressed in a shadow as Gaal mistook the shadow of a mountain as an army— "And when Gaal saw the people, he said to Zebul, Behold, there come people down from the top of the mountains. And Zebul said unto him, Thou seest the shadow of the mountains as if they were men" (Judges 9:36). Sometimes this fear is a judgment of God. Then the shaking of a leaf can frighten, "And I will set my face against you, and ye shall be slain before your enemies: they that hate you shall reign over you; and ye shall flee when none pursueth you.... And upon them that are left alive of you I will send a faintness into their hearts in the lands of their enemies; and the sound of a shaken leaf shall chase them; and they shall flee, as fleeing from a sword; and they shall fall when none pursueth" (Lev. 26:17, 36). Fear was itself a part of sin's punishment (Lev. 26:17). "The LORD shall cause thine enemies that rise up against thee to be smitten before thy face: they shall come out against thee one way, and flee before thee seven ways.... The LORD shall cause thee to be smitten before thine enemies: thou shalt go out one way against them, and flee seven ways before them: and shalt be removed into all the kingdoms of the earth.... And thy life shall hang in doubt before thee; and thou shalt fear day and night, and shalt have none assurance of thy life: In the morning thou shalt say, would God it were even! and at even thou shalt say, Would God it were morning! for the fear of thine heart wherewith thou shalt fear, and for the sight of thine eyes which thou shalt see" (Deut. 28:7, 25, 66, 67).

It has been said that *fear* is man's greatest adversary. According to an ancient legend, a man was driving one day to Constantinople and was stopped by an old woman who asked him for a ride. He took her up beside him and, as they drove along, he looked at her and became frightened and asked, "Who are you?" The old woman replied: "I am Cholera." The man ordered the old woman to get off his wagon and walk; but she persuaded him to take her along upon her promise that she would not kill more than five people in Constantinople. As a pledge of the promise she handed him a dagger, saying to him that it was the only weapon with which she could be killed. Then she added: "I shall meet you in two days. If I break my promise, you may stab me." In Constantinople 120 people died. The enraged man who had driven her to the city, and to whom she had given the dagger as a pledge that she would not kill more than five, went out to look for the old woman, and meeting her, raised the dagger to kill her. But she stopped him, saying: "I have kept my agreement. I killed only five. Fear killed the others." This legend is a parable of life. Where disease kills its thousands, fear kills its tens of thousands. The greatest miseries come from fear of trouble rather than from the presence of trouble. Fear casts its shadows throughout our lives. Fear will betray a man's spirit, break down his defense, disarm him in battle, unfit him for the work of life and add terror to his dying bed.

John tells us "fear hath torment or torture" (1 John 4:18). Thus the torment of anticipated judgment needs to be cast out. So how can David say, "Yea, though I walk through the valley of the shadow of death, I will fear no evil?" Only grace can make the difference. John wrote, "Herein is love, not that we loved God, but that he loved us, and sent his Son to be the propitiation for our sins.... Whosoever shall confess that Jesus is the Son of God, God dwelleth in him, and he in God" (1 John 4:10, 15). Sadly Christians can live under the tyranny of fear but "God hath not given us the spirit of fear; but of power, and of love, and of a sound mind" (2 Tim. 1:7). Christ has provided solace to all under his glorious domain. "We have not received the bondage again to fear; but you have received the Spirit of adoption, whereby we cry, Abba, Father" (Rom. 8:15). Consider all the messages sent by the Lord that say, "fear not."

Look at 1 John 4:18, "There is no fear in love; but perfect love casteth out fear: because fear hath torment. He that feareth is not made perfect in love." There is no fear in this love engendered by Christ. Calvin commented,

> He now commends the excellency of this blessing by stating the contrary effect, for he says that we are continually tormented until God delivers us from misery and anguish by the remedy of his own love towards us. The meaning is that as there is nothing more miserable than to be harassed by continual inquietude, we obtain by knowing God's love towards us the benefit of a peaceful calmness beyond the reach of fear. It hence appears what a singular gift of God it is to be favored with his love. Moreover from this doctrine, he will presently draw an exhortation; but before he exhorts us to duty, he commends to us this gift of God, which by faith removes our fear.

"Perfect love casteth out fear" or mature love casts fear away because the Lord has proven His love through Christ and will not fail us in time to come. God's love for us is so great that He dispossesses our fear. God does not let those who have been born from above, that is the children of God (2:29-3:1), quake with fear at the thought of the Day of Judgment. His love rips fear out by the very roots and casts it away as if it were a noxious weed. Having this fear removal from our hearts should fill us with confidence. This is the very goal that the grace of God seeks; it reaches the heart through Christ as God wipes away our sins.

Madame du Barry, the unhappy woman of the French Revolution,[*] could not resign herself to death. On the scaffold she uttered fearful yells, and cried, "O! Mr. Executioner! I pray you, one little moment!" The little moment was denied her, and her head rolled down from the guillotine, while her mouth still gaped with her dying shrieks. Oh, how different is her death compared to that of Christians. An earnest Christian woman was lying in her last illness. The disease made rapid progress, and her friends sent for the doctor about two o'clock in the morning. She was slumbering when he came, but soon opened her eyes, and said, "What brings you here, doctor; it is not your usual time to call?" The doctor said he was sent for. "Am I worse, then?" "Yes; we think you are not so well." "Am I much worse?" "I fear you are." "Well, *if this is dying, it is very easy.*" When she had finished that statement she "fell asleep in Jesus."

---

[*] Jeanne Bécu, comtesse du Barry was the last Maîtresse-en-titre of Louis XV of France [his last mistress] and one of the victims of the Reign of Terror during the French Revolution.

CHAPTER 7
I Will Fear No Evil:
Where Are We Unafraid—Walking Through the Valley of the Shadow of Death

Where do we not need to fear evil—walking through the valley of the shadow of death? "Yea, though I walk through the valley of the shadow of death, I will fear no evil" (v. 4). The very place where one would expect the greatest fear that fear is removed. David does not fear the shadow of death because he is kept by the power of the God who had redeemed him, he is escorted by the Shepherd who is Jehovah-Jesus and he is promised a dwelling place in the house of God forever. His Creator-Redeemer-God is his Shepherd who is leading him!

There are so many excellent Psalter Selections on Psalm 23. Consider this one found in Benjamin Lloyd's *The Primitive Hymns, Spiritual songs, and Sacred Poems,* #690:

> The Lord is my shepherd, no want shall come nigh,
> In pastures of verdure He makes me to lie,
> Beside restful waters he leads me in peace;
> My soul to new life he restores by his grace.
>
> In right ways He leads me for His own name's sake;

So when in the valley of death-shade I walk,
Since thou wilt be with me no ill shall I fear;
Thy rod and thy staff give me comfort and cheer.

Thou spreadest my table in face of my foes;
My head thou anointest my cup overflows,
Thy goodness and mercy pursue my life's ways;
At home with Jehovah I'll dwell endless days.

Spurgeon encapsulated this part of the verse,

Death is not the house but the porch, not the goal but
the passage to it. The dying article is called a *valley*. The
storm breaks on the mountain, but the valley is the
place of quietude, and thus full often the last days of the
Christian are the most peaceful in his whole career; the
mountain is bleak and bare, but the valley is rich with
golden sheaves, and many a saint has reaped more joy
and knowledge when he came to die than he ever knew
while he lived. And, then, it is not 'the valley of death,'
but 'the valley *of the shadow* of death,' for death in its
substance has been removed, and only the shadow of it
remains…. Death stands by the side of the highway in
which we have to travel, and the light of heaven shining
upon him throws a shadow across our path; let us then
rejoice that there is a light beyond.

David did not say there would not be any evil, but that he
will not fear evil. The last enemy death is already a
conquered foe.

"Yea [or even], though I walk through the valley of the
shadow of death, I will fear no evil." Contrast this with "She
that hath borne seven languisheth: she hath given up the
ghost; her sun is gone down while it was yet day: she hath

been ashamed and confounded" (Jer. 15:9). She had lost all her children. Her life was seemingly cut short as her sun set during the day. There was a sense of incompleteness. What a contrast she was to one accompanied by the Shepherd who is without fear, while she is ashamed and confounded. Contrast the following from Psalm 107, "Such as sit in darkness and in the shadow of death, being bound in affliction and iron; because they rebelled against the words of God, and contemned the counsel of the most High: Therefore he brought down their heart with labour; they fell down, and there was none to help" (Ps. 107:10-12). The shadow of death they were under is different than the valley of the shadow of death the sheep are under. What an illustration of one of the sheep entering the valley of the shadow of death was Stephen. He entered the valley through the impact of stones thrown at him with a demonic hatred. As stones hit him they crushed bones, soon his body was broken and splintered, he bled profusely, the face was disfigured and he called out, "Lord Jesus, receive my spirit." Just before the final blows he implored, "Lord, lay not this sin to their charge" and then he entered glory accompanied by his Shepherd who led him through that valley.

The Lord's sheep may depart this life without the opportunity of leaving a dying testimony. With some of the Lord's own there is sudden death or a mind changing illness, but there is always the accompaniment of the Shepherd.

First, What does "the valley of the shadow of death" mean? There are at least two major views of this. One view says it represents times of great distress and trial; the other view says it refers to present death. Consider with me the words of others on these two positions.

Consider what some have said of the view which says it represents times of great distress and trial. John Owen noted, "As death is the worst of evils, and comprehensive of them all, so *the shadow of death* is the most dismal and dark representation of those evils to the soul, and the valley of that shadow the most dreadful bottom and depth of that representation." Then John M. Mason proclaimed that the expression *valley of the shadow of death*, "It does not signify *dying*: for it is not the valley of *death*, but of the *shadow* of death; and the shadow of an object cannot be the same thing with the object itself." However, this can be taken another way because it can represent God's amelioration of death for the Christian. John Diodati paraphrased it, "Though I were in the terrors and dangers of present death." Jonathan Edwards wrote of "a vale overspread with a deadly shade." Others holding a similar view were Ainsworth, Calvin, Patrick, Dodd, Dickson, etc.

Consider with me the other view which refers it to present death. Thomas Scott commented, "Between that part of the flock which is on earth, and that which is gone to heaven, death lies, like a deep valley, that must be passed in going from the one to the other." C. H. Spurgeon noted, "We go through the dark tunnel of death and emerge into the light of immortality." Matthew Henry wrote, "Those that are sick, those that are old, have reason to look upon themselves as in the valley of the shadow of death. Here is one word indeed which sounds terrible; it is *death,* which we must all count upon; *there is no discharge in that war.* But, even in the supposition of the distress, there are four words which lessen the terror:—It is death indeed that is before us; but, It is but the *shadow* of death...." Thus the Lord ameliorates death or makes death, which was something unsatisfactory, better than it was originally. John Stevenson concluded, "David beautifully and poetically compares his mortal dissolution to a deep valley—a valley of dark and gloomy shadow, through which lies his road to light and rest, to life and joy. Death is indeed a valley!" Some others holding this view are Gill, Horne, Fry, etc.

An overall view of Scripture seems to suggest a combination of both views. Why? Pain and distress are called "the pains of death." Paul spoke of being "in deaths oft" (2 Cor. 11:23). And the "ways of death" speaks of the misery of wickedness here and hereafter (Prov. 14:12; 16:25). William S. Plumer wrote, "It is probable that by *shadow of death* we are several times to understand all that is dark in life and in death." John Stevenson, previously mentioned, has a good explanation,

> The 'valley of the shadow of death' is a remarkable form of expression. It is peculiar to the Holy Scriptures, and to oriental literature. It is used to represent those horrible trials, those extreme difficulties and dangers, which darken the lot of humanity. Its import in this Psalm is not however to be limited to the troubles and sufferings of active life. The Psalmist neither excludes nor overlooks these; but he rises above and beyond them all. He reaches a climax of asseveration (an emphatic declaration).... Death is the principal object in the Psalmist's view.... That Shepherd, whom he had delighted to represent as having graciously tended, and abundantly supplied, his people, he now rejoices to declare will assuredly 'comfort' them in every coming trouble, and make them more than conquerors over their last enemy.

Many saints have already entered "the valley of the shadow of death" and have arrived home. Consider in your mind's eye a valley enclosed on both sides by massive stone mountains that appear to almost meet overhead imposing an exceptionally dark shadow. Through this rocky ravine the heavenly footman guides his sheep along the path appointed in the purpose of the infinite Shepherd. Through such a valley the sheep steadily walks. The "walk" is "through the valley of the shadow of death." There is an objective at the end and a new home to be entered. Thankfully this valley is not a permanent place of travel.

Second, David did not just say *the valley of death*, **but "of the** *shadow* **of."** The curse of death which was originally pronounced on man included not only the separation of the soul from the body, but also the separation of both from God. Death at the fall was instantaneous and brought an everlasting curse. But the ever blessed Redeemer intervened between the guilty sinner and their offended God. He was declared to be "the Lamb slain from the foundation of the world" (Rev. 13:8). This intervention in time opened the way for all those for whom it was intended to enter into everlasting life. Physical death sets the redeemed free for immediate admission into the presence of God. Jesus affirmed, "Whosoever liveth and believeth in Me shall never die" (John 11:26). He also said, "He that believeth ... is passed from death unto life" (John 5:24). The penal curse of death which separates the soul from the body was once and for all cancelled through the Lord Christ's substitutionary atonement. Thus the Bible says, "Christ hath abolished death" (2 Tim. 1:10). Death was thus made ineffectual and when the believer dies it is just a dark shadow. It is death's *shadow* which means the curse of death is removed and dying grace is given. The shadow of a lion or cobra cannot hurt you. You cannot have a shadow without a bright light and the *shadow* before us is made by the eternal light of God—"God is light, and in Him is no darkness at all." And Christ is the light of the world. Christ met the substance of death but we encounter only the shadow of death. As we travel through the valley the shadow is cast from the end of the valley by the light of our Lord.

If there was a way to examine the footprints through this valley you would find that over two thousand years ago one walked through this valley with nail prints in His feet. Our forerunner went first and as the Shepherd He guides each of His through that same valley. Death is seen as a "*walk*" in the valley. Note what David said in Psalm 39:13, "before I go [or walk] hence, and be no more." A sheep follows the footsteps of his Shepherd who does not cause him to run in fear through the valley, but walks him with surety through the valley. Walking refers to a man's behavior which indicates the course of his life. Do we live in the light of the brevity of life?

Third, **Death is a walk "*through*" this valley**. The purpose is not to just go *into the valley* but *through the valley*. The Almighty Shepherd is in charge of this expedition that is assured of reaching the promised goal. "The king of terrors," indeed, may exact the accustomed tribute in passing through his dominions; and though a person has nothing wherewith to pay that tribute then he leaves behind the garment of mortality which he wears. He now has no use for it and can dispense with it, and he does not refuse to leave it behind as a pledge till in due season he return again and see it gloriously redeemed! Therefore he regards *the valley not as a place of abode*, but as *a place of passage*. Once he enters that valley he most surely passes through it. Yea, he is like one of those children of Israel walking across the swelling of Jordan, and entering safely and joyfully into the promised land called Canaan!

When Richard Baxter, the Puritan, entered the valley of the shadow of death some of his preacher friends sought to comfort him. He confessed, "I have pains; there is no arguing against sense: but I have *peace*, I *have* peace." One of those friends said, "You are now drawing near your long-desired home." His reply, "I believe, I believe." When someone asked, "How are you?" His prompt answer was, "Almost well!"

At the end of the march through the valley the sheep *do not* say, "I will *feel* no evil," but rather, "I will *fear* no evil." There are glorious prospects at the end of the valley of the shadow of death. This represents expectation. Christ has conquered death for us for He met the substance of it so that we only encounter the shadow.

John Dod (1547-1645), an eminent Puritan divine, had a violent fever and little hope that his life would be spared. However, his physician after a length of time came to him saying, "Now I have hope of your recovery." Dod answered him, "You think to comfort me with this, but you make my heart sad. It is as if you should tell one, who had been sore weather beaten at sea, and conceiving he was now arrived at the haven where his soul longed to be, that he must go back again to be tossed with new winds and waves." Dod often said in his last sickness, "I am not afraid to look death in the face; I can say, Death! Where is thy sting? Death cannot hurt me." He could say with David, "I will fear no evil." Why? For "Thou art with me."

CHAPTER 8
I Will Fear No Evil:
Why Are We Unafraid—Our Shepherd Intervenes

Why do we not need to fear evil—our Shepherd intervenes: [1] "For Thou art with me;" [2] "Thy rod and Thy staff they comfort me;" [3] "Thou preparest a table before me in the presence of mine enemies;" [4] "Thou anointest [a] my head with oil, [b] my cup runs over" (v. 5).

***First*, The reason David feared no evil was because the Shepherd is with him**. We could say this is true of all believers as well. I will not be afraid "For Thou art with me." Sheep are very timid beings and more so without their Shepherd for "a stranger will they not follow, but will flee from him: for they know not the voice of strangers" (John 10:5). This is why David said, "I will fear no evil" because his Shepherd was tending him. The source of David's courage, confidence and comfort was the presence of the Shepherd. This Shepherd has never failed His sheep. As one enters "the valley of the shadow of death" it is good to look and see Christ the Good Shepherd still at work in your behalf. Remember His work in the past? "That at that time ye were without Christ, being aliens from the commonwealth of Israel, and strangers from the covenants of promise, having no hope, and without God in the world:

but now in Christ Jesus ye who sometimes were far off are made nigh by the blood of Christ" (Eph. 2:12-13). What victory through Christ for one to be without hope and distant from God being reconciled through Christ's atoning work.

So as one considers the approach of death and the soul inquires, "How will it be?" Then you may turn affectionately to the One who has loved you with an everlasting love in atonement and hear, "There is nothing in death to harm you." Why? Because Christ "through death ... [destroyed] him that had the power of death, that is, the devil" (Heb. 2:14). So as a sheep is about to enter that valley of the shadow of death he finds he has the support of the King who destroyed the destroyer. How blessed it is to have the King of that country from which you depart and to which you go; Christ is at your side affording protection, imparting consolation, subduing fear, and inspiring hope! One declared,

> Such is the blessed privilege of the flock of the good Shepherd when called to enter the eternal world. They experience that theirs is a Royal Shepherd. He is Lord of the kingdom of grace, through which they have journeyed. He is Lord also of the kingdom of glory, upon which they are just entering.... Yea, He condescends to accompany them as they walk; and to be their guide and their guard across the unseen boundaries. The Royal Shepherd is ever with His sheep. He is not only near to them, he identifies Himself with them. He makes their cause His own. He guides them as their Shepherd—he protects them as their King—and the king of terrors flees dismayed before him. So certain does the Psalmist feel of his Shepherd's presence, that

116

he speaks of it in the present tense, as though he already experienced its comfort in the dark valley [John Stevenson].

Mrs. Elizabeth Hervey was the wife of Rev. William Hervey an American missionary to Bombay. When Elizabeth was dying a friend remarked that he hoped the Saviour would be with her as she walked through the dark valley of the shadow of death. She replied, "If this is the dark valley, it has not a dark spot in it; all is light." Most of her sick time was experienced with bright views of the perfections of God. "God's awful holiness," she said, "appeared the most lovely of His attributes." At one time she said she wanted words to express her views of the glory and majesty of Christ. She noted, "It seems that if all other glory were annihilated and nothing left but His bare self, it would be enough; it would be a universe of glory!" There was no fear with such a glorious Shepherd.

Do you remember, "Death is swallowed up in victory. O death, where is thy sting? O grave, where is thy victory? The sting of death is sin; and the strength of sin is the law. But thanks be to God, which giveth us the victory through our Lord Jesus Christ" (1 Cor. 15:54-57). Victory is in the Victor! Jonathan Edwards said, "If the sting of death is sin, victory over death must be forgiveness of sin…. The Apostle's purpose is to encourage timid Christians in the conflict against sin with the certain hope of victory at last." Christ provides victory over the wages of sin and death as well as victory over the devil. "The believer will feel the stroke of death but not the sting of death because the stinger was removed at Calvary" [D. L. Moody]. The Royal Shepherd has overthrown the king of Terrors. We are more than conquerors through King Jesus who loved us and gave

117

Himself for us (Rom. 8:37). It is said that once a bee stings you it has no more power to hurt you because its stinger is gone. Death left its stinger in the body of the man Christ Jesus and has no more power to hurt His sheep. Also, Christ's victory over the grave is our victory over death.

"For Thou art with me," is oh so consoling. He never leaves us nor forsakes us. *Remember when Paul* was in the ship that was torn by the tempestuous wind—Euroclydon? It appeared the ship would be destroyed. Paul said, "Sirs, ye should have hearkened unto me, and not have loosed from Crete, and to have gained this harm and loss" (Acts 27:21). Then Paul could say, "I exhort you to be of good cheer: for there shall be no loss of any man's life among you, but of the ship. For there stood by me this night the angel of God, whose I am, and whom I serve, Saying, Fear not, Paul" (Acts 27:22-24). The Lord was with Paul which benefited the others temporarily. Paul ended by saying, "I believe God, that it shall be even as it was told me" (Acts 27:25). What was the secret of Paul's peace facing death? The Lord was his Shepherd he did not want. *Remember when Paul* was in the imperial city surrounded by heathen enemies, forsaken by Christian friends and expecting a violent death? Paul was able to say of that, "Notwithstanding the Lord stood with me, and strengthened me; ... and I was delivered out of the mouth of the lion" (2 Tim. 4:17). *Remember when Paul* was accosted because the damsel had been delivered from demonic power and her owners lost revenue. Paul and Silas were caught and brought to the magistrates because of their exceptionally troublesome behavior in the city. The multitude tore off their clothes and commanded that they be beat. They were beaten with many stripes and thrown into prison and placed in stocks. At the midnight hour they prayed and sang praises to God. Their God sent an earthquake which shook the prison doors open and loosed everyone's chains. The jailor awoke to the situation and was about to commit suicide believing his prisoners had escaped. Paul called to him in the dark, "Do thyself no harm: for we are all here." The jailor called for a light, ran into the place where Paul and Silas were and fell down before them. Then he brought them out and said, "Sirs, what must I do to be saved? And they said, Believe on the Lord Jesus Christ, and thou shalt be saved, and thy house. And they spake unto him the word of the Lord, and to all that were in his house" (Acts 16:30-32). The point is their Lord and Saviour was with them. What was it that enabled the noble army of martyrs to be faithful unto death? It was the presence of the Great Shepherd. Read Psalm 46:1-7.

David is saying, "When in the valley of the shadow of death I fear no evil 'for Thou art with me.'" When the three Hebrew children were thrown into the fiery furnace He was with them for Nebuchadnezzar was astonished when he looked into the furnace and asked, "Did not we cast three men bound into the midst of the fire? They answered and said unto the king, True, O king. He answered and said, Lo, I see four men loose, walking in the midst of the fire, and they have no hurt; and the form of the fourth is like the Son of God" (Daniel 3:24-25). When we enter that valley of the shadow of death we have the Son of God with us! Why? "Precious in the sight of the Lord is the death of His saints" (Ps. 116:15). So precious He does not let us out of His sight!

The Lord's sheep need not fear when about to descend into the valley of the shadow of death because our Shepherd is with us. This is not a *cul de sac* but a walk through with the shadow of death hanging over. We must remember this as we have already noted, this is conquered territory by the Captain of our Salvation. What grand companionship. We have so many promises. "But now thus saith the LORD that created thee, O Jacob, and he that formed thee, O Israel, Fear not: for I have redeemed thee, I have called thee by thy name; thou art mine. When thou passest through the waters, *I will be with thee*; and through the rivers, they shall not overflow thee: when thou walkest through the fire, thou shalt not be burned; neither shall the flame kindle upon thee. *For I am the LORD thy God, the Holy One of Israel, thy Saviour*" (Isa. 43:1-3). Our Shepherd does not send a surrogate, an angel, some seraphim or cherubim for He declares to us "I will be with thee." The ministering spirits attend us only because our God is with us. Remember the comforting words of our Good Shepherd while on earth—"Lo! I am with you alway, even unto the end of the world" (Matt. 28:20). What a farewell promise. Remember the exhortation, "Be thou faithful unto death, and I will give thee a crown of life" (Rev. 2:10). Thus He is with us as our accompaniment into the land of pure delight where the throne of the Lord God is fixed.

Second, **The reason David feared no evil was because the Shepherd's rod and staff comforted him.** And we could say this is true of us as well. "Thy rod and thy staff they comfort me." The Good Shepherd is not only near His sheep in the dark valley, but He uses His means to sustain, defend and encourage them. He does not go before them at a distance and neither does He walk inattentively by their side. His "rod and His staff" are employed in bringing His sheep "comfort." As a rod, it is the Shepherd's powerful weapon of defense; and as a staff, it is

His instrument of support. Thus it is at once, therefore, the symbol of protecting power and of supporting grace.

There are multi uses of the "rod." 1st, the sheep pass under the rod for counting to insure they are all accounted for. Thus he accounts for each individual sheep so as to pursue the one that might be straying. Elizabeth Cecilia Clephane (1830-1869) wrote of this:

> There were ninety and nine that safely lay
>   In the shelter of the flock,
> But one was out on the hills away,
>   Far off in the cold and dark;
> Away on the mountains wild and bare,
> Away from the tender Shepherd's care.
>
> "Lord, Thou hast here Thy ninety and nine;
>   Are they not enough for Thee?"
> But the Shepherd made answer: "This of Mine
>   Has wandered away from Me;
> And although the road be rough and steep,
> I go to the desert to find My sheep."
>
> But none of the ransomed ever knew
>   How deep were the waters crossed;
> Nor how dark was the night which the Lord passed through
>   Ere He found His sheep that was lost.
> Out in the bleak desert He heard its cry—
> All bleeding and helpless, and ready to die.
>
> "Lord, whence are those blood-drops all the way
>   That mark out the mountain's track?"
> "They were shed for one who had gone astray
>   Ere the Shepherd could bring him back."
> "Lord, whence are Thy hands so rent and torn?"
> "They're pierced tonight by many a thorn."
>
> And all through the mountains, thunder-riven,
>   And up from the rocky steep,

121

There arose a cry to the gate of heaven,
"Rejoice! I have found My sheep!"
And the angels echoed around the throne,
"Rejoice, for the Lord brings back His own!"

2nd, the shepherd uses the rod to direct the movements of the sheep. Those that begin to lose attention in keeping up are nudged or prodded by the rod. 3rd, the rod may be used to fend off an enemy. 4th, the shepherd uses the rod to gather or collect his sheep. 5th, the shepherd rules over the flock with the rod. The rod is emblematic of the shepherds power and ownership. It is also typical of the presence and power of the Holy Spirit.

Not only the rod but he wrote the "staff comfort me." The rod may chasten me when I go astray, but the staff secures me when I fall or am about to do so. They both are for the advantage of the sheep as the Worthy Shepherd uses them. One causes me to realize my fault and error, and the other keeps me in the truth. The "staff" with its crook is used to free a sheep caught in a thicket or fallen into a pit or seized by a beast of prey. The staff is an emblem of the shepherd who comes to the relief and comfort of his flock. The staff of the Royal Shepherd is the Word of God.

The rod and staff are used by the shepherd jointly or separately as the case requires. The Lord said, "Like as I pleaded with your fathers in the wilderness of the land of Egypt, so will I plead with you, saith the Lord GOD. And I will cause you to pass under the rod, and I will bring you into the bond of the covenant" (Ez. 20:36-37). The heavenly Shepherd uses the rod of His Spirit, and the staff of His Word to sustain, direct and deliver His flock. These two instruments He uses to lead and cheer them through life. With these he upholds and comforts them in the valley of the shadow of death! The rod of His wrath is used against the disobedient (Lam. 3:1). The Lord may visit sin with the rod of correction (Ps. 89:32). When Satan would assault their soul, and try to claim them as his own, the Shepherd extends over us the "rod of his strength" (Ps. 110:2). Our Royal Shepherd "shall rule them with a rod of iron" (Rev. 2:27; 12:5; 19:15). He numbers us among the members of his little flock, and will not suffer us to be plucked out of his hand (John 10:28-30). When faith begins to decline and we scarcely discern the peaceful path through the valley, the rod of His Spirit directs us correctly, and preserves our footsteps on the straight and narrow way. "Thine ears shall hear a word behind thee, saying, This is the way, walk ye in it, when ye turn to the right hand, and when ye turn to the left" (Isa. 30:21).

When the mind is oppressed with anxious cares and the thicket of perplexity hinders our progress, the Shepherd will extricate us with the "staff" of His Word! The entanglements of this present world can distract us but His Word draws us back from those snags. Jesus declared, "These things I have spoken unto you, that in me ye might have peace. In the world ye shall have tribulation; but be of good cheer; I have overcome the world" (John 16:33). Our Shepherd said, "Peace I leave with you, my peace I give unto you: not as the world giveth, give I unto you. Let not your heart be troubled, neither let it be afraid" (John 14:27). When you fall into the slough of despondency or almost into the pit of despair your Shepherd is there with His staff and rod to apply whichever is needed. He sends the Holy Spirit with His Word into our hearts. He steadies our feeble steps. We are able to say as we go on the way, "Thy rod and thy staff they comfort me."

When Daniel Webster reached the end of his life He was visited by his friend Peter Harvey. Before the visit was over Webster said to Harvey and Marshfield, "Harvey don't leave me till I am dead – don't leave Marshfield till I am a dead man." Then as if speaking to himself, he said "On the 24th of October (1852), all that is mortal of Daniel Webster will be no more." Then he "prayed in his natural usual voice – strong, full, and clear, ending with, 'Heavenly Father, forgive my sins, and receive me to thyself, through Christ Jesus.'" From the time that he had announced to his doctor that "he should die that night," he seemed to be solicitous to recognize his advance towards the dark valley, and especially to know when he was actually entering it. "Once, being faint, he asked if he were not *then* dying? and on being answered that he was not, but that he was near to death, he replied simply, 'Well;' as if the frank and exact reply were what he had desired to receive. A little later, when his kind physician repeated to him that striking text of Scripture, 'Yea, though I walk through the valley of the shadow of death, I will fear no evil, for thou art with me; thy rod and thy staff, they comfort me,' he seemed less satisfied, and said, 'Yes; but the *fact*, the *fact* I want;' desiring to know if he were to regard these words as an intimation that he was *already* within that dark valley" [Joseph Banvard, *Life of Daniel Webster*].

The Word of God is as a "staff" used to support the living and dying believer. For example: when our Shepherd was being tempted by Satan He was supported by the Word of God which He quoted three times from Deuteronomy and Zechariah (Matt. 4:1-11). This staff is a settled matter, "For ever, O LORD, thy word is settled in heaven.... Thy word is very pure: therefore thy servant loveth it.... Thy word is true from the beginning: and every one of thy righteous judgments endureth for ever" (Ps. 119:89, 140, 160). The Worthy Shepherd uses His staff to comfort the members of His flock. David said, "Thy word have I hid in mine heart, that I might not sin against thee" (Ps. 119:11). Or his plea, "And take not the word of truth utterly out of my mouth; for I have hoped in thy judgments" (Ps. 119:43). Or "Remember the word unto thy servant, upon which thou hast caused me to hope" (Ps. 119:49). That staff of the Word is supportive, "Thou hast dealt well with thy servant, O LORD, according unto thy word" (Ps. 119:65). The sheep love the demeanor of the Shepherd's words, "How sweet are thy words unto my taste! Yea, sweeter than honey to my mouth! Through thy precepts I get understanding: therefore I hate every false way.... Thy testimonies have I taken as an heritage for ever: for they are the rejoicing of my heart.... Therefore I esteem all thy precepts concerning all things to be right; and I hate every false way" (Ps. 119:103-104, 111, 128). This staff helps us on the way, "Thy word is a lamp unto my feet, and a light unto my path" (Ps. 119:105).

Yes, this staff of the Word is the dying sheep's solace. It gives such comfort. Oh, the promissory note of Scripture, "There hath no temptation taken you but such as is common to man: but God is faithful, who will not suffer you to be tempted above that ye are able; but will with the temptation also make a way to escape, that ye may be able to bear it" (1 Cor. 10:13). Or "For God hath not appointed us to wrath, but to obtain salvation by our Lord Jesus Christ, Who died for us, that, whether we wake or sleep, we should live together with him. Wherefore comfort yourselves together, and edify one another, even as also ye do" (1 Thess. 5:9-11). With this staff we have guidance to dying—

"For this God is our God for ever and ever: he will be our guide even unto death" (Ps. 48:14). Remember those cheering words, "I will never leave thee, nor forsake thee" (Heb. 13:5). To the dying soul that is heavy laden the Shepherd of the sheep said "Come unto me" (Matt. 11:28). Remember dear flock "it is your Father's good pleasure to give you the kingdom" (Luke 12:32).

How frequently do you think that a dying believer has asked someone to read John 11? This is the consoling account of Lazarus' sickness, death, burial and resurrection. Romans 8 is declarative of the great work of God in salvation and providence. "All things work together for good to them that love God, to them who are the called according to his purpose" (Rom. 8:28 read verses 32 ff.). The resurrection chapter of the Bible is often recourse for the departing sheep (1 Cor. 15). In 2 Corinthians the dying Christian is instructed "though our outward man perish, yet the inward man is renewed day by day. For our light affliction, which is but for a moment, worketh for us a far more exceeding and eternal weight of glory; while we look not at the things which are seen, but at the things which are not seen; for the things which are seen are temporal; but the things which are not seen are eternal" (2 Cor. 4:16-18). "For we know that if our earthly house of *this* tabernacle were dissolved, we have a building of God, an house not made with hands, eternal in the heavens. For in this we groan, earnestly desiring to be clothed upon with our house which is from heaven: If so be that being clothed we shall not be found naked. For we that are in *this* tabernacle do groan, being burdened: not for that we would be unclothed, but clothed upon, that mortality might be swallowed up of life. Now he that hath wrought us for the selfsame thing *is*

God, who also hath given unto us the earnest of the Spirit. Therefore *we are* always confident, knowing that, whilst we are at home in the body, we are absent from the Lord: (For we walk by faith, not by sight:) We are confident, *I say,* and willing rather to be absent from the body, and to be present with the Lord. Wherefore we labour, that, whether present or absent, we may be accepted of him" (2 Cor. 5:1-9). They contemplate promises in Hebrews 6 and 11 about "strong consolation" and those who all died in the faith; there were those who "sought a better country, that is an heavenly." The Book of Revelation with its descriptions of heavenly worship, of heaven and eternity is the end of the staff.

The chamber of death has provided many witnesses of the Spirit and the Word or the rod and staff as the sheep depart with strong consolations. The dying have often revealed their choice comfort from Scripture for "surely I know that it shall be well with them that fear God." How precious is that declaration, "As for me, I will behold thy face in righteousness: I shall be satisfied when I awake with thy likeness" (Ps. 17:15). Oh, how tragic for those who do not have an Almighty Saviour or Divine Comforter! The sheep entering the valley say, "For I know that my redeemer liveth, and that he shall stand at the latter day upon the earth: and though after my skin worms destroy this body, yet in my flesh shall I see God: Whom I shall see for myself" (Job 19:25-27). "I will greatly rejoice in the LORD, my soul shall be joyful in my God; for he hath clothed me with the garments of salvation, he hath covered me with the robe of righteousness, as a bridegroom decketh himself with ornaments, and as a bride adorneth herself with her jewels" (Isa. 61:10). "For I am in a strait betwixt two, having a desire to depart, and to be with Christ; which is far better" (Phil. 1:23).

The sheep does not have to fear when entering the valley of the shadow of death for the Royal Shepherd will be with us all the way. The rod of His Spirit and the staff of His Word shall be used to provide comfort.

> Fear no evil then, O Christian, when thou walkest through the valley of the shadow of death. Only be faithful to thy Shepherd, and all shall be well. The light of his *presence*, the rod of his *power*, and the staff of his *promise*, shall comfort thee in that dark and trying hour. No spiritual foe shall venture to approach, when thy Shepherd's presence is vouchsafed to thee! And thou shalt assuredly experience that there is no deliverance too great for his power to accomplish; and no consolation too precious for his promise to supply, in the valley of the shadow of death" [Stevenson].

The conclusion of David regarding his Shepherd's use of His rod and staff in reference to himself was "they comfort me." What exactly is this kind of comfort? "Comfort" (*nacham*)§ is used in the sense of "consoling" and David's

---

§ The word rendered 'comfort' (from נחם *nâcham*) means properly to draw the breath forcibly, to sigh, pant, groan; then to lament, or grieve (Ps. 90:13; Jer. 15:6); then to comfort or console one's-self (Gen. 38:12). Then to take vengeance (compare the note at Isa. 1:24). All the forms of the word, and all the significations, indicate deep emotion, and the obtaining of relief either by repenting, or by taking vengeance, or by administering the proper topics of consolation. Here the topic of consolation is, that their calamities were about to come to an end, in accordance with the unchanging promises of a faithful God (Isa. 40:8), and is thus in accordance with what is said in Heb. 6:17-18.

trust in the Good Shepherd is such that His use of the rod and staff brings consolation. Why? His Jehovah-Jesus is impeccable in His usage of those instruments. Dr. John Gill explained,

> [I]t is no small comfort to the sheep of Christ that they have passed under His rod, who has told them ... that they are all numbered by Him; not only their persons, but the very hairs of their head; and that they are under his care and protection: the shepherd with his rod, staff, or crook, directs the sheep where to go, pushes forward those that are behind [or reticent], and fetches back those that go astray; as well as drives away dogs, wolves, bears, &c. that would make a prey of the flock; and of such use is the word of God, attended with the power of Christ and His Spirit....

Isaiah wrote of this kind of consolation for His people, "Comfort ye, comfort ye my people, saith your God. Speak ye comfortably to Jerusalem, and cry unto her, that her warfare is accomplished, that her iniquity is pardoned: for she hath received of the LORD's hand double for all her sins" (Isa. 40:1-2). The double use of "comfort" shows just how assured the prophet of God seeks to make God's people. Here is a confirmation and encouragement of comfort to be expected. Matthew Henry proclaimed,

> *Comfort you, comfort you* - not because the prophets are unwilling to do it (no, it is the most pleasant part of their work), but because sometimes the souls of God's people refuse to be comforted, and their comforters

must repeat things again and again, ere they can fasten anything upon them. Observe here, [1.] There are a people in the world that are God's people. [2.] It is the will of God that his people should be a comforted people, even in the worst of times. [3.] It is the work and business of ministers to do what they can for the comfort of God's people. [4.] Words of conviction, such as we had in the former part of this book, must be followed with words of comfort, such as we have here; for he that has torn will heal us.

Isaiah had much to say about comfort. "For thus saith the LORD, Behold, I will extend peace to her like a river, and the glory of the Gentiles like a flowing stream: then shall ye suck [or nurse], ye shall be borne upon her sides, and be dandled upon her knees. As one whom his mother comforteth, so will I comfort you; and ye shall be comforted in Jerusalem" (Isa. 66:12-13). Jehovah wishes to extend peace like a river to His own.

When peace, like a river, Attendeth my way,
When sorrows like sea billows roll;
Whatever my lot, thou hast taught me to say,
It is well, it is well with my soul.

Thus the Holy Spirit guides Isaiah to use the picture of a child nursing its mother's breast to illustrate "comfort." Thus the Shepherd uses the tenderest care for His sheep. The sense of security that a child has when trusting its parents issues in great consolation. Jehovah *acts* to extend peace to His people—"so will I comfort you," and His people *experience* this comfort by "being comforted." Consider the consolation of the following words, "Sing, O heavens; and be joyful, O earth; and break forth into singing, O mountains: for the LORD hath comforted his people, and will have mercy upon his afflicted. But Zion said, The LORD hath forsaken me, and my Lord hath forgotten me. Can a woman forget her sucking child, that she should not have compassion on the son of her womb? yea, they may forget, yet will I not forget thee. Behold, I have graven thee upon the palms of *my* hands; thy walls *are* continually before me" (Isa. 49:13-16). Our Shepherd poses an almost human impossibility to reinforce His care for His own when he asked if a woman breast feeding her child could forget it or cease having compassion toward that child. The point was that is a possibility with a human mother but Jehovah-Jesus declares "I will not forget thee." B. H. Carroll observed, "The sight of all this causes the prophet to call for the outburst of joy in heaven and on earth which reminds us of our Saviour's parables setting forth the joy of heaven when the sinner returns to God."

What we learn is that our Shepherd has provided for every extremity. He has already conquered death, hell and the grave for the sheep.

Third, "**Thou preparest a table before me in the presence of mine enemies**" (v. 5a). Here David writes of his awareness that he is more than Jehovah's sheep for he is also Jehovah's guest. David by the guidance of the Holy Spirit was using the metaphors that had great meaning to him, such as: being a shepherd and then his rise to being king. We are reminded by James our Lord's brother, "Every good gift and every perfect gift is from above, and cometh down from the Father of lights, with whom is no variableness, neither shadow of turning" (James 1:17).

131

1st, The covenant of salt has been enjoined by Jehovah. What does that mean? In the East this was a sacred pledge of hospitality, when men broke bread together in a person's dwelling that person pledged his protection to his guest and this was never to be violated. David and the entirety of the Lord's people are under divine protection. This covenant of salt was used to ratify agreements. This was the sign that Jehovah God had given the kingdom to David forever—"to him and to his sons by a covenant of salt" (2 Chron. 13:5). In the meat offerings they were to season the offering with salt and if they failed to do so God marked it as a failure; God who said "neither shalt thou suffer the salt of the covenant of thy God to be lacking from thy meat offering: with all thine offerings thou shalt offer salt" (Lev. 2:13). The covenant of salt was to be forever before Jehovah and His seed (Num. 18:19). Jehovah-Jesus who was David's Shepherd prepared the table before David's enemies as His stamp of approval on David.

2nd, Was there a historic event that David used to mark out this great blessing of Jehovah preparing a table before him in the presence of his enemies? David had taken his first metaphor from his past as a shepherd and next uses one from his ultimate exaltation to royalty.

Could this have reference to his tragic flight from his son Absalom and the great outpouring when he came to Mahanaim where they "Brought beds, and basons, and earthen vessels, and wheat, and barley, and flour, and parched corn, and beans, and lentils, and parched pulse. And honey, and butter, and sheep, and cheese of kine, for David and for the people that were with him to eat: for they said, The people is hungry, and weary, and thirsty, in the wilderness" (2 Sam. 17:28-29). Absalom had passed over

Jordan camping in Gilead in the area where David presently was fed from their table (2 Sam. 17:24-26).

Or could this have typical reference to the events after David's destruction of the giant Goliath and his exaltation to the royal court of Saul wherein David was detained from returning home, but kept in Saul's court where he could control David? Here David was eating at the kings table in the presence of his enemy the king (1 Sam. 18). David had gone from the sheepcote to being a brave victorious warrior and then to the court of the king. As a mere youth he had gone to stardom in the killing of the giant Goliath which led to Saul's jealousy and secret desire to kill him all the while feigning to honor him publically.

Whatever image David borrowed from to show the exalted place to which his Great Shepherd had exalted him, this was a grand honor he writes about. David's King was Jehovah God and he revels in being the King's guest. Every believing sinner in God's Son the King, as Lord and Saviour, is welcomed by the King of heaven to His royal table and none of them are turned away! Are you a regular at this table?

3rd, What kind of Host is our great God? He provides eternal salvation to His chosen guests or redeemed souls so as to purge them from sin and grant them a sumptuous feast in His glorious throne room in heaven. We are made royal banqueters.

What of these in the Old and New Testaments? Hear the comforting words, "How excellent is thy lovingkindness, O God! therefore the children of men put their trust under the shadow of thy wings. They shall be abundantly satisfied with the fatness of thy house; and thou shalt make them drink of the river of thy pleasures" (Ps. 36:7-8). "The river of pleasures" is the word "Eden" in Hebrew taking in the rivers that flowed there, but it now pictures the streams that water Paradise (Rev. 22:1-5). The God of lovingkindness also gives invitations of grace to His people, "Wisdom hath builded her house, she hath hewn out her seven pillars.... Come, eat of my bread, and drink of the wine which I have mingled" (Prov. 9:1, 5). This might be likened unto the invitation given in our Lord's parable, "The kingdom of heaven is like unto a certain king, which made a marriage for his son, And sent forth his servants to call them that were bidden to the wedding: and they would not come. Again, he sent forth other servants, saying, Tell them which are bidden, Behold, I have prepared my dinner: my oxen and my fatlings are killed, and all things are ready: come unto the marriage" (Matt. 22:2-4).

4th, What are His invitations to His own? There are wonderful invitations to believers to be ready for "The table is furnished;" "the dinner is prepared;" "the servants are sent forth;" and "all things are ready." Yes, the table is prepared in the very presence of the enemies. The use of the word "table" is comprehensive and used to refer to all kinds and sources of provisions that are needed, desirable and commensurate with the joy of the one dining as it were. The agent of this provision is Jehovah God—"Thou preparest." He is the one who provides whatever is needed to save His people. He always provides the table, its furnishings, its abundance, its satisfaction and its eternal use. Those who come to this table are invited guests and therefore bring nothing. Consider Toplady's *Rock of Ages*, Trinity Hymnal #421:

> Rock of Ages, cleft for me,
> Let me hide myself in Thee;

Let the water and the blood,
From Thy riven side which flowed,
Be of sin the double cure,
Save me from its guilt and power.

Not the labor of my hands
Can fulfill Thy law's demands;
Could my zeal no respite know,
Could my tears forever flow,
All could never sin erase,
Thou must save, and save by grace.

Nothing in my hands I bring,
Simply to Thy cross I cling;
Naked, come to Thee for dress,
Helpless, look to Thee for grace:
Foul, I to the fountain fly,
Wash me, Savior, or I die.

While I draw this fleeting breath,
When mine eyes shall close in death,
When I soar to worlds unknown,
See Thee on Thy judgment throne,
Rock of Ages, cleft for me,
Let me hide myself in Thee.

The Lord put it this way, "Ho, every one that thirsteth, come ye to the waters, and he that hath no money; come ye, buy, and eat; yea, come, buy wine and milk without money and without price" (Isa. 55:1). The word for "thirst" that Isaiah used refers to the intensity of desire showing one's anxiousness for salvation. The great thirst must be assuaged so just come to the waters freely provided by the Lord.

5ᵗʰ, What does he provide? Oh, the goodness, mercy and condescension of our God who "provides" exceeding abundantly beyond what we could ask or think (Eph. 3:20). The word "provides" means to arrange, set or put in order, set in array, prepare, order, ordain, handle, furnish, esteem, equal, direct or compare. All of God's mercies are "prepared" for His own. "Thy congregation hath dwelt therein: thou, O God, hast prepared of thy goodness for the poor. The Lord gave the word: great was the company of those that published it" (Ps. 68:10-11). That which flows from the goodness of God is provided for the poor, and the goodness of God leads to repentance (Rom. 2:4). Our God is the God of good things—"Eye hath not seen, nor ear heard, neither have entered into the heart of man, the things which God hath prepared for them that love him" (1 Cor. 2:9). He only prepares "good things" for them such as "He hath prepared for them a city" (Heb. 11:16). When the blessed Saviour left it was "to prepare a place for you" (John 14:2). When He returns "Then shall the King say unto them on his right hand, come, ye blessed of my Father, inherit the kingdom prepared for you from the foundation of the world" (Matt. 25:34). What shall He say to those who reject Him and His own—"Then shall he say also unto the on the left hand, Depart from me ye cursed, into everlasting fire, prepared for the devil and his angels" (Matt. 25:41).

6th, What are His spiritual provisions? He provides for everything needed and every contingency that arises. He extends pardon and peace, wisdom and strength, life and health, holiness and truth, comfort and sympathy, righteousness and redemption, love and joy, patience and meekness, kindness and humility, faith and hope, and care and protection. His table is laden with all good things and nothing is missing to impair its perfection. Consider how Paul's mind was filled to overflowing with gratitude in its contemplation—"Blessed be the God the Father of our Lord Jesus Christ, which hath blessed us with all manner of spiritual blessing in heavenly things by Christ" (Eph. 1:3, Tyndale's Translation). Paul is eulogizing God in this verse which is a doxology, and some say the greatest doxology. Paul begins by eulogizing God, who provided every spiritual provision—"the Creator ... is blessed for ever. Amen" (cf. Rom. 1:25; 2 Cor. 11:31). Our purpose should be "that God in all things may be glorified through Jesus Christ, to whom be praise and dominion for ever and ever. Amen" (1 Pet. 4:11). *"Blessed"* (*eulogatos*) is a word meaning to speak well of God or God is worthy of all praise. *"'Blessed'* translates an adjective used in the New Testament always of God" [Curtis Vaughan]. This eulogy or blessing toward God is frequently used in the New Testament.

> Blessed be God!—It is the song of the universe, in which heaven and earth take responsive parts. 'When the morning stars sang together and all the sons of God shouted for joy,' this concert began, and continues still through the travail of creation and the sorrow and sighing of men. The work praises the Master. All sinless creatures, by their order and harmony, by the variety of their powers and beauty of their forms and delight of their existence, declare their Creator's glory. That praise to the Most High God which the lower creatures act instrumentally, it is man's privilege to utter in discourse of reason and music of the heart" [*Expositor's Bible Commentary*].

This is the song of the Redeemed and that is the context here. Paul exudes with praise and thanks as he writes of the believer's position and present blessings enjoyed by grace. "He (Paul) ascribes all those blessings to the source of all blessing, to Jehovah, the Father, and he calls Him, 'THE

GOD AND FATHER OF OUR LORD JESUS CHRIST,'
conveying thereby the ideas included in the amazing
manifestation of His love in giving His Son to die for us, and
the unity of the divine will in the salvation of all the Church
of God" [Robert J. M'Ghee]. Note also here the three-fold
use of the same root word: "**Blessed** be the God . . . who
hath **blessed** us with all spiritual **blessings**...." The grand
object of our eulogy of praise is "the God and Father of our
Lord Jesus Christ" thus we see that He who is "our God and
Father" is also "the God and the Father" of our Lord (Eph.
1:17; John 20:17). The title is the peculiar and characteristic
designation of the Father as the God of accomplished
redemption (2 Cor. 1:3; 1 Pet. 1:3) [A. W. Pink]. Consider
the doctrine of the passage: Here the first person of the
Trinity is called both the God and the Father of Jesus. In
what sense is He the "God of Jesus Christ?" In what sense is
He the "Father of Jesus Christ?"

> God is from eternity the *Father* of the Son, but it was
> not until the word was made flesh for our salvation
> that he also became His *God* (John 20:17). And we
> are taught here to bless God for this provision of His
> grace, because it is only through the merits of *our*
> Mediator that we are brought to know God as *our*
> Father [Geoffrey B. Wilson].

Four things are said here that must be considered.

a. We have been blessed with all spiritual blessings. God
"hath blessed us" is the translation of a constative aorist
verb which sums up all the blessings of God as one grand
act and treats them as a single whole. Whatever blessings
we have, we have from God. As God alone is styled the
"Blessed One" (Mark 14:61) so as Thomas Goodwin pointed

out, "He alone blesses or is able to do so. When creatures bless they can only do so 'in the name of the Lord'" (Ps. 129:8). *"Us"* refers to Paul, the Ephesian believers and the faithful in Christ Jesus (1:1). And whatever blessings we need, he has provided. None are omitted. God is not stingy with his blessings. Contrary to what some may often think, that God is holding out on us or that there are needs in our lives we have that Christ cannot fulfill or meet, but every possible or conceivable blessing is ours.

b. These blessings are spiritual. We are "blessed ... with all spiritual blessings." The nature of our blessings are *"spiritual"* that is they are Holy Spirit produced blessings. But Paul's primary reference is to those blessings that pertain to, are characterized by, and come from the Holy Spirit himself. The word *"spiritual"* is an adjective for the Holy Spirit, and thus that pertaining to or belonging to the Spirit. What are these spiritual blessings which have been brought together? These are the blessings brought on by the Spirit that lead to life in the Spirit. Paul has particularly in mind: election, adoption, grace, redemption, forgiveness, knowledge, an inheritance, and the seal of the Spirit. Paul discusses all of these in the verses that follow. In other words, all the gifts between vv. 3 and 14 are understood as elements of this one blessing and are therefore grounds for giving praise.

c. These blessings are ours *"in heavenly places,"* a phrase found only in Ephesians (1:3, 20; 2:6; 3:10; 6:12). In 1:20 it is the sphere to which the risen Christ has been exalted and enthroned; in 2:6 it is the realm to which believers have been lifted in fellowship with Christ; in 3:10 it is where principalities and powers learn of the wisdom of God as exhibited through his people; in 6:12 it is the spiritual battleground where believers confront the forces of wickedness. Thus, the phrase "heavenly places" refers not to a physical locality but to a celestial region, a sphere of spiritual activities to which the believer has been lifted in Christ. It is not the heaven of the future but the heaven which lies *even now* within and around the Christians. Believers ... belong to two worlds (Phil. 3:20). Contrary to popular notions, the *"heavenlies"* or *"heavenly places"* one said, "does not refer to a particular location beyond our literal atmosphere, as if some celestial topography were in view, or to blessings to be enjoyed later in heaven, after one dies physically." In Ephesians this phrase can refer to (1) the place of exaltation for Christ (1:20), (2) the place of exaltation for believers because they are united with Christ (2:6), (3) the place or sphere in which God's wisdom is revealed to rulers and authorities (3:10), and (4) the place of warfare between believers and demonic forces (6:12). Thus *"the heavenlies"* are where Christ is, where those of us in Christ will be, and where God is revealed! In other words, *"heavenly realms"* does not refer to a physical location but to a spiritual reality, God's world, in which believers have a share and which evil forces still seek to attack. It includes all of the believer's relation to God. It is a way of saying that this world is not the only reality. A larger reality exists where Christ is already exalted as Lord, where believers participate in his victory, and where spiritual forces are opposed. Heavenly places, therefore, is a reference to the world of spiritual reality. It is the unseen, spiritual realm in which we enjoy God's presence, commune with Jesus, and wage war with the enemy. The child of God has a temporary relation to the earth, but he has an eternal relation to heaven.

d. These blessings are only available *"in Christ."* This phrase may well be the most important theological theme in Paul's writings. This concept occurs twelve times in the first fourteen verses of Ephesians chapter one and occurs 164 times in Paul's writings. As we were once *"in Adam"* who represented us as *"in sin,"* by what he did, we were reckoned fallen in Adam, so now we are represented *"in Christ"* (Rom. 5:19; 1 Cor. 15:22). "You cannot be a Christian without being *'in Christ,'* Christ is the beginning as well as the end. He is Alpha as well as Omega. There are no blessings for Christians apart from him" [D. M. Lloyd-Jones]. Believers are chosen in Christ, redeemed in Christ, accepted in Christ, and in our text we are blessed in Christ. This means that the blessings which we experience come to us by virtue of our union with Christ. He represents us. What was said of Christ can now be said of believers (cf. 2:6). Christ is the person in whom believers reside, the source in which they find God's salvation and blessings, and the framework in which they live and move and have their being. As we have just seen all the blessings of salvation are provided as God's provision for His own. The Lord provides the lawbreaker a pardon through Christ (Titus 3:5). Thus the pardon has been procured, the Holy Spirit has been given, the Bible has been published, the table has been prepared and the sinner is invited to come (remember Isa. 40:1-2 and Luke 14:21-22).

7th, The table has not been set for the future but the table is prepared "before me" said David. We can say the table is prepared "before us." Our salvation is not far off but shall not tarry; it is already ours (Isa. 46:13). "O taste and see that the LORD is good: blessed is the man that trusteth in him" (Ps. 34:8). Jesus said, "Man shall not live by bread alone, but by every word that proceedeth out of the mouth of God" (Matt. 4:4). There is also a promise of Jesus, "And I appoint unto you a kingdom, as my Father hath appointed unto me; That ye may eat and drink at my table in my kingdom, and sit on thrones judging the twelve tribes of Israel" (Luke 22:29-30, 16). The redeemed have been saved, are being saved and shall be saved. They are filled with joy and gladness. "And an highway shall be there, and a way, and it shall be called, The way of holiness; the unclean shall not pass over it; but it shall be for those: the wayfaring men, though fools, shall not err therein. No lion shall be there, nor any ravenous beast shall go up thereon, it shall not be found there; but the redeemed shall walk there: And the ransomed of the LORD shall return, and come to Zion with songs and everlasting joy upon their heads: they shall obtain joy and gladness, and sorrow and sighing shall flee away" (Isa. 35:8-10). Why such joy? Consider all the "fear not's" that have been spoken to them. "Fear not" God has heard your voice (Gen. 21:17), fear not I am with you (Gen. 26:24), fear not the Lord is with us (Num. 14:9), fear not I have redeemed you (Isa. 43:1), fear not little flock (Luke 12:32), fear not I am the first and the last (Rev. 1:17).

"Thou preparest a table"—Behold, the King! "Thine eyes shall see the King in his beauty" (Isa. 33:17). "Look upon Zion, the city of our solemnities ... but there the glorious LORD will be unto us a place of broad rivers and streams; wherein shall go no galley with oars, neither shall gallant ship pass thereby. For the LORD is our judge, the LORD is our lawgiver, the LORD is our king; he will save us.... The people that dwell therein shall be forgiven their iniquity" (Isa. 33:20-24).

Remember Christ has gone to prepare a place for us and come and take us to be with Him where He is (John 14:3). Remember Lazarus and the rich man? Lazarus the poor beggar died and the angels carried him into Abrahams bosom [the reclining position in East when eating, like the disciples at the supper] or to be with Abraham in Paradise; the rich man also died and in hell lifted up his eyes being in torment. He saw Lazarus reclining at Abraham's chest at the meal (Luke 16:22-23). The rich man cried out for help, "Father Abraham, have mercy on me, and send Lazarus, that he may dip the tip of his finger in water, and cool my tongue; for I am tormented in this flame" (Luke 16:24). But he was reminded of his lifetime of good things the very opposite of Lazarus, and he was reminded of the impossibility of anyone bridging the great gulf (Luke 16:25-26).

Yes, Lord, you prepare a table before me in the presence of my enemies. Thanks Lord!

Fourth, "**Thou anointest [a] my head with oil, [b] my cup runs over.**" As we just saw Jehovah-Jesus prepared a table for David in the presence of his enemies. What a glorious provision with our Lord's table abundantly laden with good things, but it does not end there for the abundance of the oil of gladness covers the head and the overflowing cup in his hand also represents the great provisions of our Royal Shepherd. This part of the verse gives a special mention of the honors bestowed upon David and the abundance provided for his enjoyment by the King of Heaven. Both these pictures are borrowed from oriental custom. Thus there was an anointing of the person as an honored guest and the placing into his hands a cup that was brimming over with its contents.

Captain James Wilson in his *Memoirs* described such an event in his own life: "I once had this ceremony performed on myself in the house of a great and rich Indian, in the presence of a large company. The gentleman of the house poured upon my head, my hands, and arms, a delightful, odoriferous, perfume. He then put a golden cup into my hands, and poured wine into it, till it ran over; assuring me at the same time, that it was a great pleasure to him to receive me, and that I should find a rich supply in his house." So it was that Wilson received an assurance of acceptance, abundance and hospitality.

David, by the Holy Spirit's guidance, appealed to this cultural custom which was well known in the East. This custom was prevalent in the hot climate for it met a need for refreshing the guests received as well as providing a sweet smell to the entire house. The guest was honored in a distinct way and supplied with abundance under the roof of his host. This custom involved a profusion of costly perfumes or fragrances of oils.

> Anointing the head with oil is, therefore, an emblem of happiness arising from the kindest offices of friendship. Scriptural usage applies it to the Holy Spirit, who is, emphatically, *the oil of gladness*, wherewith the Savior Himself was *anointed*, and with which he anoints the heads of His people. In other words, the Holy Spirit who rested without measure upon the Lord Jesus, and by this *measureless* communication of all divine gifts and graces, constituted Him the CHRIST, the ANOINTED, rests likewise upon all the members of his ... body; communicating to them out of his fullness, a suitable *measure* of gifts and grace [James M. Mason].

1. David said that Jehovah anointed his head with oil. What a great honor to have the Redeemer-Creator God to provide such a pleasant benefit. The anointing or unction is from the Holy One. The word "anointed" in the Old Testament is the word *Messiah* (Heb. *Masiah*) and in the New Testament it is the word *Christ* (Gk. *Christos*) and is applied to the Redeemer primarily and secondarily to the believer because of the union with Christ. He is called *"Christ,"* because He is *the anointed one*: and all his true disciples, after Him, are rightly denominated *"Christians,"* because they are *anointed ones*. The Spirit of God abundantly poured upon our great High Priest, was "like the precious ointment upon the head, that ran down upon the beard, even Aaron's beard, that went down to the skirts of his garments" (Ps. 133:2). The children of the Lord are distinct from the children of the world. John the apostle wrote, "But ye (children) have an unction from the Holy One, and ye know all things" (1 John 2:20).

King Saul may have shown David such royal favor to acknowledge him publically as the giant killer and the king's guest, but this was miniscule in comparison with the Royal Shepherd who anointed him with "the oil of gladness" or "the joy of the Holy Spirit!" Just think of the following contrast: the anointing oils of Egypt (the picture of the world) were used to preserve dead bodies, but the anointing oil of Jehovah in grace poured out this oil that flowed from the head throughout the soul in purification to spiritual life.

The holy child Jesus was anointed (Acts 4:27). Our blessed Anointed One the Christ was so dishonored by one Simon [not Simon Peter] who did not anoint His head or show proper hospitality [just think of our own country and the disrespect to God and His Son]. Consider Luke's account: "And one of the Pharisees desired him that he would eat with him. And he went into the Pharisee's house, and sat down to meat. And, behold, a woman in the city, which was a sinner, when she knew that *Jesus* sat at meat in the Pharisee's house, brought an alabaster box of ointment, And stood at his feet behind *him* weeping, and began to wash his feet with tears, and did wipe *them* with the hairs of her head, and kissed his feet, and anointed *them* with the ointment. Now when the Pharisee which had bidden him saw *it,* he spake within himself, saying, This man, if he were a prophet, would have known who and what manner of woman *this is* that toucheth him: for she is a sinner. And Jesus answering said unto him, Simon, I have somewhat to say unto thee. And he saith, Master, say on. There was a certain creditor which had two debtors: the one owed five hundred pence, and the other fifty. And when they had nothing to pay, he frankly forgave them both. Tell me therefore, which of them will love him most? Simon answered and said, I suppose that *he,* to whom he forgave most. And he said unto him, Thou hast rightly judged. And he turned to the woman, and said unto Simon, Seest thou this woman? I entered into thine house, thou gavest me no water for my feet: but she hath washed my feet with tears, and wiped *them* with the hairs of her head. Thou gavest me no kiss: but this woman since the time I came in hath not ceased to kiss my feet. My head with oil thou didst not anoint: but this woman hath anointed my feet with ointment. Wherefore I say unto thee, Her sins, which are many, are forgiven; for she loved much: but to whom little is forgiven, *the same* loveth little. And he said unto her, Thy sins are forgiven. And they that sat at meat with him began to say within themselves, Who is this that forgiveth sins

146

also? And he said to the woman, Thy faith hath saved thee; go in peace" (Luke 7:36-50).

One of the primary lessons we learn from this passage: "Thou anointest my head with oil" is that David lived a life of awareness of His unseen God who created, redeemed, anointed and preserved him. David eclipsed the earthly honors of being anointed for his heart was set on the heavenly anointing of Jehovah. Remember the great question that Jesus asked, "How can ye believe, which receive honour one of another, and seek not the honour that cometh from God only" (John 5:44)? The point of this verse is that Jesus having pointedly reproved their unbelief then as a good physician pointed to the cause; they did not value Christ because they overvalued themselves. David had received human accolades when he killed Goliath but that was nothing compared to his Jehovah God who was his strength and salvation and Shepherd and Anointing God. All David's honors were, as he knew, ultimately from the Lord his heavenly King who anointed his head with oil. "David had already enlarged on his security and blessedness as a believer, under the beautiful similitude of a sheep with its shepherd. He now contemplates, by this new figure, the honor to which as a believer he was exalted" [John Stevenson].

This act of his Heavenly Host was very humbling to David who knew his sinfulness and depraved nature, but he could rejoice in full and free grace. The Psalmist wrote, "Thy throne, O God, is for ever and ever: the scepter of thy kingdom is a right scepter. Thou lovest righteousness, and hatest wickedness: therefore God, thy God, hath anointed thee with the oil of gladness above thy fellows" (Ps. 45:6-7).

147

At Oriental feasts oil was poured on the heads of distinguished and very welcome guests; God himself anoints the man Christ Jesus, as he sits at the heavenly feasts, anoints him as a reward for his work, with higher and fuller joy than any else can know; thus is the Son of man honoured and rewarded for all his pains. Observe the indisputable testimony to Messiah's Deity in Ps. 45:6, and to his manhood in the present verse. Of whom could this be written but of Jesus of Nazareth? Our Christ is our *Elohim*. Jesus is God with us. [C. H. Spurgeon].

The anointing of God's Son precedes the anointing of the adopted sons of God. The glorious Host in heaven condescended to bestow such a glorious anointing. David has grasped what this means and that is, life is a feast and the Lord's own are His guests. This Host is glad to confer His blessings though costly to Himself to show us that we are accepted in the Beloved (Eph. 1:6). Here is reference to David's son yet David's Lord (Matt. 22:42 ff.). Jesus was anointed with the Holy Spirit (Acts 10:38). In Matthew's Gospel we are told that a "king made the marriage supper" (Matt. 22:2, 4). Then there is the marriage of the Lamb (Rev. 19:7, 9). Our acceptance to the marriage supper is as a result of being His "friends"—"Greater love hath no man than this, that a man lay down his life for his friends" (John 15:13). As a token of this love each invited guest is anointed—"Now he which stablisheth us with you in Christ, and hath anointed us, is God; Who hath also sealed us, and given the earnest of the Spirit in our hearts" (2 Cor. 1:20-21). Thus we have the earnest or guarantee of the Spirit and thus an unction from the Holy One (1 John 2:20). The apostles witnessed the resurrected Christ and His seating at the right hand of God and Holy Spirit's promise (Acts 2:33).

Anointing oil was prescribed by Jehovah for physical use (Ex. 30:22 ff.). Therefore, every vessel and every priest used in the service of God was anointed with oil. The High Priest, the kings and the prophets were consecrated by pouring the holy anointing oil on the head. Oil and its qualities are a great lesson spiritually as oil was a symbol of the Holy Spirit. The eternal Spirit proceeded from the Eternal Father and was bestowed on the Beloved Son and was poured out upon the body of Christ. As oil penetrates, softens, heals, strengthens and preserves so also it will gladden, consecrate, adorn, render fragrant and illuminate. Thus in all these various and important properties it represents to us the powers, offices, gifts and graces of the Holy Spirit. The Holy Spirit in like fashion is indispensable to life and vigor, to holiness and happiness, for every believing soul.

Are we praying for a spiritual anointing? Yes, we are unworthy and only the Holy Spirit can freely answer such a prayer. Everyone who asks, seeks and knocks receives (Luke 11:9-10). Jesus asked, "If ye then, being evil, know how to give good gifts unto your children: how much more shall your heavenly Father give the Holy Spirit to them that ask him" (Luke 11:13)? God the Holy Spirit anoints like oil which penetrates the inmost soul, softens hard hearts, heals spiritual wounds, illuminates darkened understandings and strengthens our godly resolutions. The anointing Spirit consecrates believers to serve God, fills them with joy unspeakable, adorns them with holiness and causes them to be fragrant with odors of righteousness. Christ makes us as sweet perfume unto God the Father (2 Cor. 2:15). What a position to be in as we previously noted—"Thy God, hath anointed thee with the oil of gladness above thy fellows" (Ps. 45:7). "I have found David my servant; with my holy oil have I anointed him" (Ps. 89:20). As Gill noted this was the Holy Spirit being referred to as the holy oil. David declared personally of Jehovah—"Thou anointest my head with oil."

2. David said that his cup was running over. We were earlier introduced to this cultural custom. David had been under the hospitality of his Royal Shepherd as a table was prepared for him in the presence of his enemies and as his head had been anointed by the Master of the feast, and now as a cup was put into his hand and poured full to overflowing. A cup brimming over with wine was symbolical of complete hospitality. Thus David pictures his Heavenly Host making this provision for him thus securing his place under His care.

Please note also the figurative use of the term "cup" in Scripture. Commonly we either have a "cup of sorrow" or a "cup of joy." When David wrote of the punishment of the wicked at God's hand he said, "The LORD trieth the righteous: but the wicked and him that loveth violence his soul hateth. Upon the wicked he shall rain snares, fire and brimstone, and an horrible tempest: this shall be *the portion of their cup*" (Ps. 11:5-6). When David described the blessedness he experienced he declared, "The LORD is the *portion* of mine inheritance and of *my cup*: thou maintainest my lot" (Ps. 16:5). Thus when David speaks in our text he explained, "my cup runneth over" which is harmonious with a banquet provided by his God.

The overflowing cup represents to our minds a great generosity which the King of heaven has provided for His people. This is not a measured quantity, but an unmeasured and overflowing fullness which the supply of the Lord. David writes in a brief but expressive language that may be considered in a two-fold respect: referring to an abundance both of temporal mercies and of spiritual blessings. The whole sense is applicable to the two-fold nature of the believer, so that he is enabled with all the emphasis of truth to declare, both as to his body and as to his soul, "My cup runneth over."

Just contemplate David's great benefactor who is also by grace ours. The God of all, He is our Shepherd. C. H. Spurgeon proclaimed,

> I feel as if I could stop preaching and fall to repeating the words, 'Mine own God,' 'Mine own God,' for the Lord is as much my God as if there were no one else in the world to claim him. Stand back ye angels and archangels, cherubim and seraphim, and all ye hosts redeemed by blood! Whatever may be your rights and privileges, ye cannot lessen my inheritance. Assuredly all of God is mine—All his fullness, all his attributes, all his love, all himself, all, all is mine, for he hath said, 'I am thy God.' What a portion is this! What mind can compass it? O, believer, see here your boundless treasure! Will not your cup run over now? What cup can hold your God? If your soul were enlarged and made as wide as heaven you could not hold your God; and if you grew and grew and grew till your being were as vast as seven heavens, and the whole universe itself were dwarfed in comparison with your capacity, yet still you could not contain him who is infinite. Truly, when you know by faith that Father, Son, and Spirit are all your own in covenant, your cup must run over.

The overflowing cup is not dependent on our capacity for receiving or what we deserve! We receive the fullness of grace and truth through Jesus Christ for in Him "we received, and grace for grace" (John 1:16). Yes, it is the furnisher of the feast who puts into our hand this cup overflowing, "For it pleased the Father that in him should all fullness dwell; And, having made peace through the blood of his cross, by him to reconcile all things unto himself; by him, I say, whether they be things in earth, or things in heaven" (Col. 1:19-20). Thus we see that in Christ "all fullness dwells." In ourselves we have nothing; but in Christ we have salvation which supplies as much grace and glory as to cover us for time and eternity and above that if needed. Our cup overflows because all things are ours in Christ (1 Cor. 3:22-23). In Christ "dwelleth all the fullness of the Godhead bodily. And ye are complete in him, which is the head of all principality and power" (Col. 2:9-10). Thus the grace supplied in Christ is immeasurable and inexhaustible. This cup has endless supply. In Christ is contained the fullness of the Godhead bodily and this cup is exhaustless.

Think of the fact that God the Father is for you in salvation; that God the Son is for you in salvation; and that God the Holy Spirit is for you in salvation! Yes, the cup overflows! "What shall we then say to these things? If God *be* for us, who *can be* against us? He that spared not his own Son, but delivered him up for us all, how shall he not with him also freely give us all things? Who shall lay any thing to the charge of God's elect? *It is* God that justifieth. Who *is* he that condemneth? *It is* Christ that died, yea rather, that is risen again, who is even at the right hand of God, who also maketh intercession for us. Who shall separate us from the love of Christ? *shall* tribulation, or distress, or persecution, or famine, or nakedness, or peril, or sword? As it is written, For thy sake we are killed all the day long; we are accounted as sheep for the slaughter. Nay, in all these things we are more than conquerors through him that loved us. For I am persuaded, that neither death, nor life, nor angels, nor principalities, nor powers, nor things present, nor things to come, Nor height, nor depth, nor any other creature, shall be able to separate us from the love of God, which is in Christ Jesus our Lord" (Rom. 8:31-39). Truly the cup runneth over! We are more than conquerors through Christ.

Who could calculate all the benefits and blessings which flow from this cup? For our great Shepherd provides life from the dead, sight for the blind, deliverance for the captives, food for the hungry, water for the thirsty, riches for the poor, robes of righteousness for the naked in sin, rest for the weary, relief for the oppressed, strength for the weak, instruction for the ignorant, peace for the troubled and consolation for the afflictcd! By His grace we are brought under the conviction of sin, shown Christ as redeemer, given repentance toward God, experience sorrow over our sin, deliverance through the blood of Christ and are kept by the power of God unto salvation ready to be revealed in the last time. What have we received from this cup of joy? We have been made new creatures in Christ, the children of God, brethren in Christ, temples of the Holy Spirit, fellow citizens with the saints, heirs of salvation, joint heirs with Christ, a chosen generation, a peculiar people, a royal priesthood, and more than conquerors through Christ. Time would fail to tell of all the overflowing cups of the saints (Heb. 11:32 ff.). Spurgeon commented,

"The fuller a vessel becomes the deeper it sinks in the water."

> My shepherd is the Lamb,
> The living Lord, who died!
> With all that's truly good, I am
> Most plenteously supplied!
> He richly feeds my soul
> With manna from above.
> And leads me where the rivers roll
> Of everlasting love
>
> He seeks me when I stray:
> Directs my every path:
> And when I walk through death's dark way
> Draws near with rod and staff.
> My table he doth spread
> In presence of my foes:
> With oil He doth anoint my head:
> My cup with wine o'erflows.
>
> Goodness and mercy wait
> On all my steps through life
> They'll bear me to the heavenly gate,
> And set me free from strife.
> Then I my Shepherd's care
> Shall praise; my Host adore:
> And in his Father's house shall share
> True bliss for ever more.

What did it cost Christ that your cup might overflow in grace and salvation? He must drain the cup of God's wrath against you! "This cup" had to be faced and consumed. The *"cup"* was an idiom which the Hebrews used to refer to the wrath of God, and the punishment He sends upon sin (cp. Ps. 75:8; Isa. 51:17, 22; Jer. 25:15; 51:7). As Isaiah proclaimed, "When thou shalt make His soul an offering for sin" (53:10), for His "soul was heavy unto death" (Matt. 26:38). The intensity of this substitutionary work was great. John Flavel said that Christ

> [H]ad no relief ... not a drop of comfort came from heaven into His soul to relieve it, and the body by it: but, on the contrary, his soul was filled up with grief, and had an heavier burden of its own to bear than that of the body; so that instead of relieving, it increased unspeakably the burden of its outward man.

The wrath of God came upon Jesus' soul. The cup contained the portion of sorrows to be drunk including all the dregs in the cup, which the Father distributed. "Upon the wicked he shall rain snares, fire, and brimstone, and a horrible tempest; this shall be the portion of their cup" (Ps. 11:6 cp. Ez. 23:32-35). The portion of their cup was the punishment allotted to them by God for their wickedness, and this is what Jesus drank for all those for whom He suffered and died. Consider what the Lord Christ had to drink, "For in the hand of the LORD there is a cup, and the wine is red; it is full of mixture; and he poureth out of the same: but the dregs thereof, all the wicked of the earth shall wring them out, and drink them" (Ps. 75:8). Here was the disclosure of the contents of the cup. As has been noted previously this was the cup of God's wrath against sin. However, look at the contents of the cup more closely.

[a] The cup contained the anger of God against those who have violated His holy law and who seek to destroy His holy kingdom. How is God's anger against sin expressed?

155

"God is jealous, and the LORD revengeth; the LORD revengeth, and is furious [the sense of the Hebrew word 'furious' is that this is a permanent feeling]; the LORD will take vengeance on His adversaries, and He reserveth wrath for His enemies. The LORD is slow to anger, and great in power, and will not at all acquit[1] the wicked: the LORD hath His way in the whirlwind and in the storm, and the clouds are the dust of His feet.... Who can stand before His indignation? And who can abide in the fierceness of His anger? His fury is poured out like fire, and the rocks are thrown down by Him" (Nahum 1:2, 3, 6).

This is a portion of that cup. The Lord Jesus had to be sustained or this anger would have consumed Him.

[b] The cup contained the pure wrath of God. Not a drop of mercy or comfort was mixed, but wrath without mercy. "The same shall drink of the wine of the wrath of God, which is poured out without mixture into the cup of his indignation; and he shall be tormented with fire and brimstone in the presence of the holy angels, and in the presence of the Lamb: And the smoke of their torment ascendeth up for ever and ever," (Rev. 14:10-11). The Lord Jesus had to drink such a cup so we could be exempted and our cup run over—"For God spared not His own Son" (Rom. 8:32). "For the wrath of God is revealed from heaven against all ungodliness and unrighteousness of men" (Rom. 1:18). The non-believer has "the wrath of God abiding on him" (John 3:36). But why does the believer not have "the wrath of God abiding on him?" The reason is the Lord Jesus drank the cup of the pure wrath of God. If he had not

---

[1] Will not hold guiltless, will not clear or treat as innocent and will not release.

done so we would have been subject to it. Thus our cup runs over with the joy of salvation rather than damnation.

[c] The cup contained all the wrath of God against all the sins of all the elect. This is beyond what a sinner suffers, because the sinner suffers for his own sins, but the Lord Jesus had the sins of a multitude which no man can number (Rev. 7:9). This prevents the believer, who has the imputed righteousness of Christ, from feeling one drop of wrath. He thus laid down His life for the sheep. God the Father "poured out His [Jesus Christ's] soul unto death: and He was numbered with the transgressors; and He bare the sin of many, and made intercession for the transgressors" (Isa. 53:12). Christ Jesus in consuming this cup eliminates the vindictive wrath of God from any chastening of His people in time. The soul suffering Christ drained the dregs (cp. Ps. 75:8).

[d] The cup contained the aggravated wrath of God that was beyond the sufferings of those in hell. How can this be true? No one in hell was ever in the relationship as the beloved of God, "This is My beloved Son in whom I am well pleased" the Father said. No one in hell had the capacity to endure such wrath as Christ. This is what made His soul sufferings so intense. No one in hell was innocent as the Lord Jesus who received the wrath of God for the sins of so many others. "And He made His grave with the wicked, and with the rich in His death; because He had done no violence, neither was any deceit in His mouth. Yet it pleased the LORD to bruise Him; He hath put Him to grief: when thou shalt make His soul an offering for sin" (Isa. 53:9-10).

Truly the Messiah was "cut off, but not for Himself" (Dan. 9:26). The Lord Jesus completely drank the cup of God's fury, even the dregs, in our behalf (cp. Isa. 51:17, 22,

23). What a glorious Saviour! Yes, our cup runs over with the fruits of Christ's righteousness.

What did it cost Christ that your cup might overflow in grace and salvation? He must drain the cup in the garden and on the cross! "O My father, if it be possible let this cup pass from me" (Matt. 26:39). What caused Christ such agony in the garden? The *"cup"* was filled with wrath against sin. This "crying and tears" was directed "unto Him that was able to save Him from death." The object of our Lord's plea was God the Father, who alone had the ability or power to meet the request, and the One to whom His all was entrusted. This does not mean "to save Him from death" on the cross or physical death, but it means soul death. The reference is not natural death, but soul death from the curse of the law (Gal. 3:13), for in the garden His soul was heavy unto death. This prayer "was heard."[2] When Jesus entered the garden he cast Himself upon the mercy of His Father as the burden became overwhelming. In this prayer he requested, "O My Father, if it be possible let this cup pass from me..." (Matt. 26:39). The object of this prayer was that "this cup pass from Him" but always with the stipulation that the Father's will be done. Was Jesus asking for His body to be kept alive so He would not be brought to crucifixion? Was the Lord Jesus asking to be let off the hook and escape the suffering substitutionary work in redemption? A thousand times no! John A. Broadus explained,

---

[2] εισακουσθεις is an aorist passive participle from εισακουω. "He was heard insofar as He desired to be heard; for although He could not but desire deliverance from the whole, as He was man, yet He desired it not absolutely as the God-man, as He was wholly subject to the will of the Father." John Owen, see *Hebrews*, Vol. 4, 509.

'If it be possible' i.e. morally possible, consistent with the Father's purpose of saving men. The God-man speaks according to his suffering human nature, referring all to the Father (cp. 20:23; Mark 13:32). In Mark (14:36) the expression is stronger, 'All things are possible unto thee … but what thou wilt' he refers it to the Father's *will*.

This possibility that was brought up was not physical because "with God all things are possible" (Matt. 19:26), but as Broadus pointed out, this is speaking morally. It was not possible for the cup to pass unconsumed! Why? The grand reason was that God the Father had pledged His eternal love to His saints by solemn decree (Eph. 1:4-5), and the Son of God had purposed before the foundation of the world to suffer and die for those the father had given Him. "If it be possible" but it was not possible any more than it was possible for the elect to be deceived (Matt. 24:24). The man Christ Jesus was of one person with the Son of God so all of his obedience was the obedience of God; however, He had a distinctness of being, and His will was distinct from that of the Father. Jesus had a will of His own. He did not want his will done but He wanted His Father's will done, and it was so (Matt. 26:39). However, since this cup could not pass and the agony of soul was so great an angel came from the Father's throne to strengthen Jesus so that His soul and body would be equipped for all that was necessary for redemption to be accomplished (Luke 22:43). There was a sense that Jesus was preserved from death in the garden so He could go to the cross in fulfillment of Scripture. The presence of the angel was an indication that this cup could not pass away, and His body was to be sustained in order to be sacrificed upon the cross. Evidently Jesus had to be sustained, because in the garden experience He would bleed through His forehead, which is not common suffering under any circumstance.

It was also the bitter cup which hc was soon after to drink on the cross. The sufferings which Christ underwent in his agony in the garden were not his only sufferings; though they were so very great. But his last sufferings upon the cross were primary sufferings; and therefore they are called "the cup that he had to drink." The sufferings of the cross, under which he was slain, are always in the Scriptures represented as the main sufferings of Christ; those in which especially "he bare our sins in his own body," and made atonement for sin. His enduring the cross, his humbling himself, and becoming obedient unto death, even the death of the cross, is spoken of as the main thing wherein his sufferings appeared. This is the cup that Christ had set before him in his agony.

It is manifest that Christ had this in view at this time, from the prayers which he then offered. According to Matthew, Christ made three prayers that evening while in the garden of Gethsemane, and all on this one subject, the bitter cup that he was to drink. Of the first, we have an account in Matt. 26:39. "And he went a little farther, and fell on his face and prayed, saying, O my Father, if it be possible, let this cup pass from me; nevertheless, not as I will but as thou wilt:" of the second in verse 42, "He went away again the second time and prayed, saying, O my Father, if this cup may not pass from me, except I drink it, thy will be done:" and the third time was in verse 44, "And he left them, and went away again, and prayed the third time, saying the same words." From this it becomes plain as to what it was of that Christ had such terrible views and apprehensions at that time. What he thus insists on in his prayers, shows on what his mind was so deeply intent. It was his sufferings on the cross, which were to be endured the next day, when there should be darkness over all the earth, and at the same time a deeper darkness over the soul of Christ, of which he had now such lively views and distressing apprehensions. Yes, the Son of God drank the bitter cup that our cup might overflow.

David could say "my cup runneth over" and that was a statement of his Shepherd's complete hospitality toward him. And this can be claimed by all the Lord's children by grace.

Section 3

David Confessed: Jehovah-Jesus is My Shepherd Therefore I Shall Dwell in the Lord's House Forever

CHAPTER 9
I Shall Dwell in the House of the Lord Forever:
Therefore David Concluded His Future Was in Good Hands

We have been considering in Psalm 23 David's "Confession." *First*, David confessed: Jehovah-Jesus is My Shepherd therefore I shall not want (vv. 1-3). *Second*, David confessed: Jehovah-Jesus is My Shepherd therefore I will fear no evil (vv. 4-5). *Third*, David confessed: Jehovah-Jesus is My Shepherd therefore I shall dwell in the house forever (v. 6). Now we come to consider this last verse in this glorious Psalm.

David by divine inspiration wrote, "Surely goodness and mercy shall follow me all the days of my life: and I will dwell in the house of the LORD forever" (v. 6). [1] David concluded that since Jehovah-Jesus was his Shepherd his future was in good hands—"Surely goodness and mercy shall follow me all the days of my life," and [2] David had a certainty that since Jehovah-Jesus was his Shepherd his eternal home was secure—"I will dwell in the house of the LORD forever." The second will be considered in chapter 10.

First, David concluded that since Jehovah-Jesus was his Shepherd his future was in good hands—"Surely goodness and mercy shall follow me all the days of my life." Here we shall find Goodness and Mercy personified; they are always accompanying the children of God in every facet of their lives for the Lord promised—"I will never leave thee, nor forsake thee" (Heb. 13:5). The times of deepest testing, the times of greatest joy, the times of heartbreaking sorrow, the times of glorious worship, the times of questioning providences, the times of adoring praise are all encompassed. It would be better to contemplate the accompaniment of Goodness and Mercy! Why? So that our murmurs might be put to silence, so that our tumults might be turned to tranquility and that our joy might blossom into its eternal form. The prospect set before the Lord's sheep is not only that Jehovah-Jesus goes before them as their Shepherd but He has, as it were, put two of His sheep dogs to guard the rear. They are named Goodness and Mercy.

Goodness and Mercy are the guardians of Jehovah-Jesus' sheep. There will never come a time when the Lord's people will be left without the Lord's protectors and messengers. Goodness and Mercy got us started on the heavenly way and together they will see us safe to glory. Yes, even ministering angels are watching over the Lord's sheep (Heb. 1:14).* Some say that Goodness and

---

* A. W. Pink commented, "Think of it, the unfallen angels waiting upon the fallen descendants of Adam! The courtiers of Heaven ministering to worms of the earth! The mighty angels, who 'excel in strength,' taking notice of and serving those so far beneath them! Could you imagine the princes of the royal family seeking out dwellers in the slums and ministering to them, not once or occasionally, but constantly? But the analogy altogether fails. The angels of God are sent forth to minister unto redeemed sinners! Marvel at it.

It should awaken within us fervent praise to God. What an evidence of His grace, what a proof of His love that He sends forth His angels to 'minister' unto us! This is another of the wondrous provisions of His mercy, which none of us begin to appreciate as we should."

Mercy are two ministering angels, and another has said they are God's appointed footmen. Remember the two angels that came to Sodom to bring Lot, Abraham's nephew, out before the Lord destroyed the place. Remember that here is something better than the help of angels! What is that? The personified attributes of God are His goodness and mercy, which is God Himself. Goodness is not alone for we are sinners needing mercy to help. No! Mercy is not alone for we need much more from the Lord. Goodness supplies our needs and Mercy forgives us. Does goodness provide and mercy pardon? Notice David's use of these attributes when he wrote, "The LORD is good; His mercy is everlasting" (Ps. 100:5). Jehovah's goodness is sure and His mercy is unending toward His people. Upon review of his past history and present experience David concluded that his Shepherd provided for him "all the days of his life." Thus his hope for the future was certain because of the immutability of his God, God's faithfulness to His promises, and His omnipotence to carry out His purposes. Yea, his God was in all His attributes and acts arrayed in his behalf.

Consider God's Goodness: The English word "God" is from the original Saxon meaning "The Good." Webster noted that "God" and "*good* are written exactly alike in Saxon, it has been inferred that *God* was named from his *goodness.*" God is the chiefest good. The goodness of God is comprehensive of His attributes. Thus when God revealed Himself to Moses taxing Moses' mortality He said, "I will make all my goodness pass before thee" (Ex. 33:19) as if divine goodness were a fountain of all the other streams of His glory. We are not referring to God's primary perfection which is His holiness or to His fullness in Himself, but we are referring to the bounty of God, His charitableness and liberality in His management of all things [Stephen Charnock]. He also explained that when God's goodness is turned into a license to sin then God turns that goodness into justice. God's goodness is underived as the essence of divine nature. God was "eternally good before there was any communication of His bounty, or any creature to whom it might be imparted or exercised. Thus, the first manifestation of this divine perfection was in giving being to all things. 'Thou art good, and doest good' (Ps. 119:68). God has in Himself an infinite and inexhaustible treasure of all blessedness enough to fill all things" wrote A. W. Pink. Everything that emanates from God is good as "God saw that everything that he had made, and, behold, it was very good" (Gen. 1:31). Thomas Manton, the Puritan minister and scholar, said that God is "originally good, good of Himself, which nothing else is; for all creatures are good only by participation and communication from God." Consider "the riches of his goodness" and "the goodness of God leadeth thee to repentance" (Rom. 2:4).

God's goodness is manifested in His creation, redemption and providence. *His goodness was seen in His creation.* "The LORD is good to all: and his tender mercies are over all his works" (Ps. 145:9). What should the goodness of God in creation cause us to do? It should lead us to exclaim, "O LORD our Lord, how excellent is thy name in all the earth!... What is man, that thou art mindful of him" (Ps. 8:1, 4). *God's goodness was demonstrated in redemption* as He gave His only begotten Son as the substitutionary sacrifice for all the elect. How is this goodness revealed in redemption? "God commendeth his love toward us, in that, while we were yet sinners, Christ died for us" (Rom. 5:8). That goodness was seen in the gift of Christ. Jesus said, "I am come that they might have life, and that they might have it more abundantly" (John 10:10). *God's goodness is evident in providence.* Paul at Lystra spoke of this goodness in providence—"He did good, and gave us rain from heaven, and fruitful seasons, filling our hearts with food and gladness" (Acts 14:17). Oh, how evident is this attribute even among the animals, "That thou givest them they gather: thou openest thine hand, they are filled with good" (Ps. 104:28). Compare His goodness, "If ye then, being evil, know how to give good gifts unto your children, how much more shall your Father which is in heaven give good things to them that ask him" (Matt. 7:11)? Our God loves to show His goodness. His goodness in providence is seen in testing times—"God ... will not suffer you to be tempted above that ye are able; but will with the temptation also make a way to escape" (1 Cor. 10:13). God in His providence prepares His people in life and for eternity.

David declared, "Oh how great is thy goodness, which thou hast laid up for them that fear thee; which thou hast wrought for them that trust in thee before the sons of men" (Ps. 31:19). He also said, "I had fainted, unless I had believed to see the goodness of the LORD in the land of the living" (Ps. 27:13)! He also said, "The earth is full of the goodness of the LORD" (Ps. 33:5). How long will God's goodness last? "The goodness of God endureth continually" (Ps. 52:1). God's goodness ought to be an attribute that is praised—"Oh that men would praise the LORD for His goodness" (Ps. 107:8, 15, 21, 31). Four times in Psalm 107 he mentions the need for such praise.

Consider God's Mercy: "Mercy is His darling attribute, which He most delights in" and "Mercy sweetens all God's other attributes," said Thomas Watson. What is meant by mercy? Our God is the merciful God who comes to help His creation in their misery. Mercy is the result of God's goodness. Mercy is another communicable attribute. "Mercy is that adorable perfection in God by which He pities and relieves the miserable" explained Robert Haldane. Mercy flows from the fountain of grace and bears the fruit of peace. Mercy is the Lord's delight—"He delighteth in mercy" (Micah 7:18). Mercy is part of the Lord's wealth—"God, who is rich in mercy" (Eph. 2:4).

No one deserves mercy because we have a sin nature and actively sin deserving the wrath of God. You can bring God's judgment upon yourself but you cannot make Him show you mercy. God may love us freely (Hosea 14:4), may save us freely (Eph. 2:8-9), may elect us freely (Eph. 1:4), may justify us freely (Rom. 3:24), may show mercy freely (Titus 3:5). Mercy is the Lord's meeting place—"I will commune with thee from above the mercy-seat" (Ex. 25:22). It is because of Jehovah's mercies that we are not consumed (Lam. 3:22). There is general and special mercy. God's general mercy extends to all His works including unconverted people for "His tender mercies are over all His works" (Ps. 145:9; Matt. 14:14; Mark 6:34). God's special mercy is extended to those He chose in Christ before the foundation of the world. Thus by God having mercy on His elect He brings them to a state whereby they are called "vessels of mercy, which he had afore prepared unto glory" (Rom. 9:23). Special mercy is for the elect alone and bestows upon them compassion as victims of sin. This is described as great mercy (1 Kings 3:6), plenteous mercy (Ps. 86:5), abundant mercy (1 Pet. 1:3), rich mercy (Eph. 2:4) and everlasting mercy (Ps. 103:17). Yes, God's mercy endures forever and this phrase is repeated twenty-six times in Psalm 136.

This is a distinguishing mercy. "This attribute could be marked out from other qualities that are similar, as grace, love, longsuffering. These attributes had much in common with mercy, yet they were distinguished. Grace viewed man as a person without merit.... So mercy is involved with that demerit; mercy is the great development of the love of God. Mercy is not the exercise of a divine attribute like God's power or His wisdom, which cost God nothing. The act of mercy is always costly. This is unlike the act of mercy of an earthly prince or king pronouncing pardon. It cost the death of His only begotten Son. It was mercy that gave birth to the Son of God; it was mercy that clothed the Son of Man as the 'Man of sorrows' in shame and blood on Calvary's cross" [Peter Connolly].

Goodness and Mercy are following us as we walk by faith and not by sight (2 Cor. 5:7). God's goodness is a matter of faith—"O taste and see that the LORD is good: blessed is the man that trusteth in him" (Ps. 34:8). We here see the promise of that for our eyes are on the Shepherd who garrisons us with His sheep dogs dear old Goodness and Mercy. Yes, we could say how gracious for "goodness and mercy shall follow." Following our Great Shepherd is an exercise of faith and then being followed is an encouragement. What a glorious thing is grace for even when we walk through the shadow of death we are not alone for our Good Shepherd is with us even then. Tyndale translated, "Faith is a sure confidence of things which are hoped for, and a certainty of things which are not seen.... But without faith it is unpossible to please him. For he that cometh to God, must believe that God is, and that he is a rewarder of them that seek him" (Heb. 11:1, 6). What constitutes the exercise of faith? Please consider the contents and foundation of this faith.

[1] Consider the contents of faith in exercise for there is a secure testimony of God's providence. David had been led into green pastures and beside still waters. Then he looked up to see the valley of the shadow of death and he had been given faith to realize that he would "walk through" that valley. Then he scanned the horizon and saw his multitude of enemies but by faith he also enjoyed a table that Jehovah-Jesus, his Shepherd, had prepared for him the very presence of those enemies. His enemies were manifold for they were from without, such as the Philistines and others and from within, involving family members as well as other leaders among his people. And now he realizes that these enemies could not take him from behind because when he glanced back there was Goodness and Mercy. They could not take him in time for Jehovah-Jesus was his Shepherd guarding him with rod and staff, and they could not take him in death for as he walked through the shadow of death Jehovah-Jesus was with him and he was unafraid, and they could not take him after death for he would be dwelling in the house of the Lord forever.

[2] Consider the foundation of this faith. "Other foundation can no man lay than that is laid, which is Jesus Christ" (1 Cor. 3:11). David's walk exercises an implicit trust that regardless of his unworthiness Goodness and Mercy will never be withdrawn. How does he know? The assurance of this very Psalm which the Holy Spirit led him to write, for Goodness and Mercy "shall follow me all the days of my life." This strong belief is based on the strong foundation of the promise of God his Shepherd—"For the gifts and calling

172

of God are without repentance" (Rom. 11:29). If the Shepherd should fail His sheep this would not be true. My Shepherd-Saviour-Redeemer is Jehovah who does not change—"For I am the LORD, I change not; therefore ye sons of Jacob are not consumed" (Mal. 3:6). Since this is true the sheep are not consumed or forsaken. Remember "It is of the LORD's mercies that we are not consumed, because his compassions fail not. They are new every morning: great is thy faithfulness. The LORD is my portion, saith my soul; therefore will I hope in him. The LORD is good unto them that wait for him, to the soul that seeketh him" (Lam. 3:22-24).

Not only are Goodness and Mercy following but they are "surely" doing so. "Surely" or "emphatically," David declared they are back there! He had no doubt in his mind. It would be gross presumption and vile ingratitude to doubt Jehovah-Jesus' Word. David's confidence was not in himself but in his unchangeable God. There is nothing fickle about this truth. Spurgeon concluded: "This is a fact as indisputable as it is encouraging and therefore a heavenly verily, or 'surely' is set as a seal upon it.... These twin guardian angels will always be with me at my back and my beck. Just as when great princes go abroad they must *not* go unattended, so it is with the believer." Why is David so sure? God is sovereign, all knowing, all powerful, everywhere present, etc. It is "sure" because God has never failed in the past, will not fail in the present and shall not fail in the future.

Our surely or surety is also a person—the Lord Jesus Christ, who is the surety of a better covenant (Heb. 7:22). A surety is one who undertakes to pay another's debt because he insured payment. It was an ancient custom for a surety to give his hand or strike hands with the other person's creditor (Job 17:3; Prov. 6:1). Thus a "surety" is one who pledges himself to pay another's debt. One who cannot discharge his own obligations needs a surety. The need for a surety implies a failure and the surety is the one who stands in the place or stead for that person who failed to pay. This is illustrated in Genesis 43:8-9, "And Judah said unto Israel his father, send the lad with me, and we will arise and go; that we may live, and not die, both me and thou, and also our little ones. I will be *surety* for him; of *my* hand shalt thou require him: if I bring him not unto thee, and set him before thee, then let *me* bear the blame forever." Yes, Judah became surety for the lad (Gen. 44:32-33). Paul volunteered to be a *surety* for Onesimus: "If he hath wronged thee, or oweth thee ought, *put that on mine account*; I Paul have written it with mine own hand, *I will repay*" (Philemon 18-19). This is exactly what Jehovah-Jesus did for His people. Sins are by analogy called "debts," for as a debt obliges the debtor to pay, so sin requires that the sinner be punished in payment. Christ, as our surety, underwent the penalty of the violated law when He offered up Himself a sacrifice to satisfy divine justice, and reconcile us to God. And as a consequence of the substitutionary atonement Jesus made sacrifice of Himself by the Holy Spirit to pay off the sin debt of all for whom He died. Our cry should be the cry of the Psalmist, "Be surety for thy servant for good" (Ps. 119:122).

A surety, whose name is put into a bond, is not only bound to pay the debt, but he makes it his *own* debt also, even as well as it is the principal's, so that *he* may be sued and charged for the debt. So Christ, when He once made Himself a surety, He so put Himself in the room of sinners, that what the law could lay to their charge, it might lay to His" [Thomas Goodwin].

Christ took our guilt of sin before He took our punishment so as to satisfy Divine justice on our behalf. Christ owned our sins as His own (Heb. 10:5-13). Jesus "Who his own self bare our sins in His own body on the tree" (1 Pet. 2:24). Those in Christ have great prospects. "Surely goodness and mercy shall follow me all the days of my life: and I will dwell in the house of the LORD forever" (Ps. 23:6).

CHAPTER 10

I Shall Dwell in the House of the Lord Forever:
Therefore David Concluded His Eternal Home Was Secure

Remember David by divine inspiration wrote, "Surely goodness and mercy shall follow me all the days of my life: and I will dwell in the house of the LORD forever" (v. 6). As we previously noted: [1] David concluded that since Jehovah-Jesus was his Shepherd his future was in good hands—"Surely goodness and mercy shall follow me all the days of my life," and now we consider that [2] David had a certainty that since Jehovah-Jesus was his Shepherd his eternal home was secure—"I will dwell in the house of the LORD forever."

Second, **David had a certainty that since Jehovah-Jesus was his Shepherd his eternal home was secure**—"I will dwell in the house of the LORD forever." This is a glorious prospect that the Holy Spirit uses to end this Psalm. Here are the prospects of the believers hope and future privileges by grace. David has showed the extraordinary amount of comfort he enjoyed with such a Shepherd. His future prospects were even more extensive. Yes, David is in an eternal fold and banqueting room with his heavenly Host the Royal Shepherd. His faithful

Shepherd and heavenly Host shall eternally receive his worship while he dwells in the house of the Lord forever.

David's strong conviction! By way of introduction David had a strong conviction regarding his dwelling in Jehovah's house. This had been David's desire—"One thing have I desired of the LORD, that will I seek after; that I may dwell in the house of the LORD all the days of my life, to behold the beauty of the LORD, and to enquire in his temple" (Ps. 27:4). Yes, this was David's "desire in prayer" that extended throughout his life. He was a man of purpose for *"one thing"* he begged or enquired of the Lord. Remember Jesus said to Martha that she was "troubled about many things: But *one thing* is needful: and Mary hath chosen that good part, which shall not be taken away from her" (Luke 10:41-42). David aimed for that which would not be taken away. Remember the rich young ruler whom Jesus told, "Yet lackest thou *one thing*: sell all that thou hast, and distribute unto the poor, and thou shalt have treasure in heaven: and come, follow me. And when he heard this, he was very sorrowful: for he was very rich" (Luke 18:22-23). Earthly treasure was the *one thing* the rich young ruler desired, but David's aim was to the contrary. An act of the Lord can change the *one thing*, *"one thing* I know, that, whereas I was blind, now I see" (John 9:25). This unfailing thing—"But one thing has never failed—one thing makes me feel that my life has been *one*; it has calmed my joys, it has soothed my sorrows, it has guided me in difficulty, it has strengthened me in weakness. It is the *presence* of God—a faithful and loving God," [George Wagner]. Spurgeon commented, "The man of one book is eminent, the man of one pursuit is successful. Let all our affection be bound up in one affection, and that affection set upon heavenly things."

The *one thing* that David desired of the Lord was the very thing he would "seek after." His holy purpose and single mindedness was translated into resolute action. What was the end result of that resolute action? David said, "That I may dwell in the house of the Lord all the days of my life." To "dwell" is to make permanent abode. Remember the widow Anna—"And she was a widow of about fourscore and four years, which departed not from the temple, but served God with fastings and prayers night and day" (Luke 2:37). She was a primary example of what a widow should be. How did she use her eighty-four years as a widow? We are told how she spent her life after the death of her husband. She did not withdraw, feel sorry for herself, re-marry or become a spreader of idle tales (1 Tim. 5:11-13). This does not mean that remarriage is wrong, except to say that the will of God for her was not in remarriage. Actually she had a love for the house of God where she spent eighty-four years, and she loved to behold the beauty of the Lord and to enquire in His temple. There she waited for Christ Jesus "the consolation of Israel." Remember when Jesus' disciples observed Him ascending into heaven—"And they worshipped him, and returned to Jerusalem with great joy: And were *continually in the temple*, praising and blessing God" (Luke 24:52-53).

David desired that he might steadfastly attend the public service of God with other faithful Israelites. He desired to do the will of God regarding public worship. He was tired of war and its consequences. He did not desire to shirk his duties as the Lord's servant responsible to rule His people. What he longed for was to not be rushed in life and be able to do his duty to God and men. Remember how Hezekiah, a son of David, desired the recovery of his health that he might *go up to the house of the Lord* (Isa. 38:22).

All God's children desire to dwell in God's house; where should they dwell else? Not to sojourn there as a wayfaring man, that turns aside to tarry but for a night, nor to dwell there for a time only, as the servant that abides not in the house forever, but to dwell there all the days of their life; for there the Son abides ever. Do we hope that praising God will be the blessedness of our eternity? Surely then we ought to make it the business of our time, [Matthew Henry].

David's love for the house of God was evident during his years as shepherd and king. He desired his Father's house in time and he was assured that he would go to his Father's house in eternity. First consider his relationship with the house of God in life before considering it in death.

David's desire to dwell or remain in the house of the Lord all of his days was "to behold the beauty of the LORD." There is a great deal of difference in the true worship of God and man centered worship. "Beauty" in its true state is an overwhelming and breath-taking thing in the spiritual and physical realm. Much that passes for worship today is the improvised pseudo-beauty of the flesh and not of the Spirit. Here it is "the beauty of the LORD."

This *'beauty'* is the Lord's well-pleased look; such a look as the Father gave, when his voice proclaimed, 'This is my beloved Son, in whom I am well-pleased.' It also means all that makes God an object of affection and delight to a soul. Nothing could be more desirable to Christ, than this approving look of his Father, telling, as it did, his love to the uttermost. And nothing to us sinners can equal this look of love; it is the essence of heaven now, and heaven for ever, [Andrew A. Bonar].

Oh, what beauty to a saved sinner is the love of Christ, the personal sufferings of Christ in our behalf, the glorious Father in heaven who gave His Son to earth and offered Him a sacrifice for our sins, the glorious Spirit of God who came in regeneration and conversion to bring to salvation those the Father gave the Son and for whom the Son died. "Out of Zion, the perfection of beauty, God hath shined" (Ps. 50:2).

Consider David's certainty. Now to come back to our text wherein David certifies by the Holy Spirit where he will spend eternity—"I will dwell in the house of the LORD forever." Here are David's prospects by transforming grace. Thus his God in mercy opened up earthly and eternal prospects. A house of worship and a home in heaven are divine provisions. Imagine a home where death cannot enter, where loved ones are never separated and where friendships are never parted! Every conceivable happiness is comprehended in this expression, "the house of the Lord." What single privilege for time or for eternity remains beyond it to be desired? David with a full heart sums up his joy and this Psalm together when he said, "And I will dwell in the house of the LORD for ever!" Oh, how blessed, how glorious are the privileges the Lord confers on His believing people! He admits them into His gracious presence in His congregation on earth, and He will receive them into His glorious presence in His congregation in heaven.

What is David's final desire? The very last of all the blessings which David wrote about was his great desire to enjoy the Lord's house. He could not contemplate a happier home, brighter bliss or greater joy than being in the home and heart of his heavenly Father! Thus with gladness of heart, gratefulness of spirit and determination of mind David exclaimed, "I will dwell in the house of the LORD for ever!" Dwelling in a house implies our admission to family intimacy and friendship with the Father. Remember when David said, "I was glad when they said unto me, Let us go into the house of the LORD" (Ps. 122:1). David, like all God's children, is a constant worshipper before the throne of God in time and will be for eternity. What a privilege to come into His presence with thanksgiving and into His court with praise and bless the name of the Lord (Ps. 100:4).

What does "the house of the LORD" mean? The "house of the LORD" denotes the presence of Jehovah in His dwelling place; this is the place where as our Father He meets with His people. This was obvious in David's words in Psalm 27:4 where he desired to seek after the Lord and dwell in His house all the days of his life, to see Him in His beauty and to inquire in His temple. God's house on earth formed the object of David's regard. The import of "the house of the LORD" is that it is the dwelling place of the Most High God. Remember how the cloud of His presence covered the Tabernacle and the brightness of His glory shone in the sanctuary. God's dealing with His people through His servants and messages were connected with the place of worship. The place of worship is where God and His children meet. This meeting was through an intercessor, through atonement for sin, and for the worship of the eternal God. Remember when Jacob received the vision of Jacob's ladder and he awakened out of sleep and said, "Surely the LORD is in this place; and I knew it not. And he was afraid, and said, How dreadful (or to be reverenced) is this place! This is none other but the house of God, and this is the gate of heaven" (Gen. 28:16-17). Jehovah settled the kind of worship, the place of worship and the attitude of worship which is acceptable. "For the LORD hath chosen Zion; he hath desired it for his habitation. This is my rest for ever: here will I dwell; for I have desired it" (Ps. 132:13-14). Our Lord in wisdom has selected the body of Christ as His church. Thus He has provided a temple of truth, a place of peace, a vestibule of heaven, a sanctuary for the soul, etc. His house is built on the Rock of Ages, with the walls of salvation and the gates of praise. This is a garden of Eden.

What is the house of God called? It is called the city of God (Heb. 12:22), the heavenly Jerusalem from above (Gal. 4:26), the shepherds fold (John 10:16), a chaste virgin to Christ (2 Cor. 11:2), the Lamb's wife (Rev. 21:9), the body of Christ (Eph. 1:22-23; Col. 1:18), the house of God, the church of the living God, the pillar and ground of the truth (1 Tim. 3:15), etc. What have the Lord's people become? They have become heirs of God, joint heirs with Christ, members of Christ's body, partakers of the Divine nature and one with God forever (Rom. 8:17; Eph. 5:30; 2 Pet. 1:14; John 17:21). They are people of the happy family of the Lord for they worship the same Father, they trust in the same Saviour, they enjoy communing with the same Spirit and they speak with one heart, voice and soul.

Who dwells in the house of the Lord? David declared that he would dwell in the Lord's house. Consider the following verse, "But Christ as a son over his own house:

whose house are we, if we hold fast the confidence and the rejoicing of the hope firm unto the end" (Heb. 3:6). As Moses was faithful in all his house (Heb. 3:5) so Christ is faithful over His house, but Moses' faithfulness was finite and temporal while Christ's faithfulness was infinite and eternal. Christ was as a Son over His own house. He has "Absolute and supreme authority over all persons and things is intended in this expression. All persons belonging unto the house of God are at His disposal, and the institution of the whole worship of it is in His power alone" [John Owen]. The believer is a part of the house or body of Christ. These believers are "holy brethren, partakers of the heavenly calling" (Heb. 3:1). Their proof of belonging to the house of Christ was their perseverance in the most holy faith. Paul wrote, "Now therefore ye are no more strangers and foreigners, but fellow-citizens with the saints, and of the household of God" (Eph. 2:19). The child of God by grace is a part of God's household. We are living stones in a spiritual house—"Ye also, as lively stones, are built up a spiritual house, an holy priesthood, to offer up spiritual sacrifices, acceptable to God by Jesus Christ" (1 Pet. 2:5). Those who are living stones are also a chosen generation, a royal priesthood, an holy nation, a peculiar people worshipping or praising Him (1 Pet. 2:9). These are also described as epistles of Christ, lambs of His flock, sheep of His fold, salt of the earth, lights of the world, pillars in His temple, a peculiar treasure, jewels in His crown and a royal diadem in His hand (2 Cor. 3:3; John 21:15-16; Matt. 5:13-14; Rev. 3:12; Ps. 135:4; Mal. 3:17; Isa. 62:3). The people of the Lord were slaves of the world who were by saving grace turned into free men, citizens of heaven, kings and priests unto God (1 Cor. 7:22; Phil. 3:20; Rev. 1:6). They are satisfied—"Blessed is the man whom thou choosest, and causest to approach unto thee, that he may dwell in thy courts: we shall be satisfied with the goodness of thy house, even of thy holy temple" (Ps. 65:4). Remember David was glad when they said to him, "Let us go into the house of the Lord." The house of God is where "the times of refreshing shall come from the presence of the Lord" (Acts 3:19).

Oh, the glories of the house of the Lord. Here the weary pilgrim has found rest, here the lonely stranger has reached home, here the good and faithful servant hears "well done," here the runners of the race have "finished their course with joy," here the contender receives "the prize of the high calling," here the prayer warrior has "prevailed with God," here the soldier of Christ has "fought a good fight ... and finished their course," here the soldier of Christ has received the "crown of righteousness," here the little flock fears not for it is "the Father's good pleasure to give them the kingdom," here the poor find "treasure in heaven" (an "inheritance in light," "fullness of joy," and "an eternal weight of glory") and here those who are weeping find that "God shall wipe away all tears from their eyes."

The length of time David said he would spend in the Lord's house was "forever." All God's people have "passed from death unto life." They finish their course and live with their Father forever.

What did Jesus say about the house of the Lord? "My Father's house" comes from the very words of our Lord Jesus Christ in John's Gospel chapter 14. "My Father's house" was the Lord Jesus' way of introducing the subject. The Father's house should be our desired destination once our lost estate is settled and Christ Jesus is our Salvation. Yes, when the time of our departure comes our prospects are gloriously bright if we are headed to the Father's house. David asserted, "I will dwell in the house of the LORD for ever," and this shows it was settled with him.

Jesus' words, as recorded by John, are glorious: "Let not your heart be troubled: ye believe in God, believe also in me. In my Father's house are many mansions: if *it were* not *so,* I would have told you. I go to prepare a place for you. And if I go and prepare a place for you, I will come again, and receive you unto myself; that where I am, *there* ye may be also.... Peace I leave with you, my peace I give unto you: not as the world giveth, give I unto you. Let not your heart be troubled, neither let it be afraid" (John 14:1-3, 27). Thus this dwelling place is prepared by the Prince of Peace. Jesus was saying to His own, "You can stop being agitated or troubled of heart since I am going away (John 13:33) just keep on believing in God the Father and Me." Jesus simultaneously declared that believing in God the Father and in Him was correct. This also shows the divinity of Christ as an object of believing unto salvation. Then He referred to His "Father's house" where there were many places to dwell, and if that were not so I would tell you. Then the promise was given, "I go to prepare a place for you" which indicates this is a special eternal home personalized for each inhabitant. Then Jesus said "if I go and prepare a place for you" and I am going, I will return to get you and take you unto Myself for the purpose of you being with Me "where I am." This is very reminiscent of Stephen's experience at his stoning as he saw heaven open and the son of Man standing on the right hand of God to receive him (Acts 7:55-56). "And they stoned Stephen, calling upon God, and saying, Lord Jesus, receive my spirit"

(Acts 7:59). Stephen died and his soul went immediately to glory.

Did you notice the promises made regarding Jesus' Father's house? It has many mansions. It is certain—"If it were not so, I would have told you." It has Jesus' personal touch—"I go to prepare a place for you." It is the entrance into the valley of the shadow of death where no evil is feared because "I am with you;" and Jesus asserted, "I will come again, and receive you unto Myself." It is a glorious place for it is "where I am," said Jesus and "there ye may be also." This passage is called Jesus' *Farewell Discourse* to His disciples. Later in the chapter Jesus said to His own, "Peace I leave with you, my peace I give unto you: not as the world giveth, give I unto you. Let not your heart be troubled, neither let it be afraid" (John 14:27).§ Also, we need to remember the Scriptural teaching on the new heaven and new earth and new Jerusalem.‡

We should remember that the Father's house is where the Father is in all His glory. We should remember that the Lord is honored there and His people delight in Him. We should remember it is a holy place not made with hands and is eternal. We should remember it is a sinless place that shall never be polluted with sin for its inhabitants are righteous in Christ. We should remember it is a place where rest remains for the people of God and it is without pain, sorrow or weariness. We should remember it is paradise and a return to Edenic times without the possibility of another fall in Adam. We should remember it is a glorious home where we are with our Father, our Elder Brother and our Sanctifier God the Holy Spirit. We should remember

§ See Appendix 2
‡ See Appendix 3

that this is our eternal home where all the family of God is gathered and we dwell in the house of the Lord together forever!

We may sing, study and sanctify this Psalm to our hearts for it is glorious and comforting. David sang this Psalm first long long ago. Therein he wrote and sang of the Shepherd who cared for His sheep and David was one of them. The Shepherd undertook for that sheep to bring it back into the earthly fold where a table had been prepared but there were even greater prospects for that sheep for it was to eternally reside in the Father's house. Can you say with David, "LORD I have loved the habitation of thy house, and the place where thine honour dwelleth" (Ps. 26:8)?

Appendix 1

C. H. Spurgeon's Reading Comments on Psalm 23

I hope we all know this Psalm by heart, may we also know it by heart-experience! It is a sweet pastoral song just suited to our Sabbath evening worship. There is here no din of arms, no noise of war; but there is a delicious hush, only broken by the gentle tinkling of the sheep-bell. God give us that sweet rest tonight!

Verse 1. *The LORD is my shepherd;*

All true rest begins with Jesus, as all the comfort of the sheep is provided for their by their shepherd.

"The Lord is my shepherd." Is it so? Canst thou look up, poor defenseless sheep, and say, "The Lord is my shepherd"? Then comes the blessed inference:

Verse 1. *I shall not want.*

I do not want, I cannot want; I never shall want with such a Shepherd as I have. He will provide for me; nay, more, God himself is my provision. All I need I have, for "The Lord is my shepherd, I shall not want." I cannot provide for myself, but I shall not want. Famine may come, and others who have no God to go to, may pine and perish, but in the worst season I shall not want, for "The Lord is my shepherd."

Verse 2. *He maketh me to lie down in green pastures:*

I am so weak that I even need God's help to enable me to lie down, but "He maketh me to lie down." Yes, the rest of the soul is so hard to attain that nobody ever does reach it except by the power of God. He who made the heavens must make us to lie down if we are really to rest. What delightful rest it is when we lie down in his pastures, which are always green! Did you ever find them dry? Our Shepherd makes us not only to feed, but so to feed that we lie down in the midst of the pastures. There is more than we can eat, so the Lord makes a couch of it for us: "He maketh me to lie down in green pastures:"

Verse 2. *He leadeth me beside the still waters.*

There is, first, contemplation: "He maketh me to lie down." Then there is activity. "He leadeth me." There is also progress, and there is provision for our advance in the heavenly way: "He leadeth me." He leadeth me beside the waters of quietness, not by the rushing torrents of excitement, nor by the place of noisy strife. "He shall not strive, nor cry, neither shall any man hear his voice in the streets." "He leadeth me beside the still waters." Not, he drives, or drags; but he himself leads, going first to show the way. It is for me to follow, happily to follow, where "He leadeth me beside the still waters."

Verse 3. *He restoreth my soul:*

He can do it at once. He restoreth now. He is a restoring God. "He restoreth my soul." He brings my wandering spirit back when I forsake his ways; and having done that, he leads me, even more carefully than before, for a second time we have the psalmist's declaration, "He leadeth me."

Verses 3-4. *He leadeth me in the paths of righteousness for his name's sake. Yea, though I walk through the valley of the shadow of death, I will fear no evil:*

Though death's shadow hovers all around me, and damps my spirit, though I feel as though I must die, and cannot bear up under present trial any longer, "Yea, though I walk," for I do walk I will not quicken my pace, I will not be in a flurry, I will not run for it. Though death itself shall overshadow me, I will keep up my walk with God. Though I walk through the valley of the shadow of death, I will fear no evil." There is none, therefore I will not fear any. We often feel more afraid through our fear itself than through any real cause for fear. Some people seem to be ever on the lookout for fear where there is none. Do not you see any, nor let any enter your heart; gay with the psalmist, "I will fear no evil:"

Verse 4. *For thou art with me;*

Should a sheep fear when the shepherd is with it? What cause has it to fear if that Shepherd is omniscient, omnipotent, and full of tenderness?

Verse 4. *Thy rod and thy staff they comfort me.*

Thy rule and thy correction: thy rod, with which I sometimes am made to smart; thy staff, with which I am supported. These are my comforts; why should I fear? Are you drinking in all this precious truth, dear friends? Are you feeling it in your soul's deepest experience? This Psalm is very good to read, but it is far better to write out from your own experience. Make it a song of your own; not merely a song in the Book, but a song for yourselves.

Verse 5. *Thou preparest a table before me in the presence of mine enemies:*

There is a fight going on, and there are enemies all around. You do not generally have tables set in the hour of battle; but God keeps his people so calm amid the bewildering cry, so confident of victory, that even in the presence of their enemies a table is spread with all the state of a royal banquet. "Thou preparest a table." There is a doth on the table, there are the ornaments on it, and there are all the accompaniments of a feast: "Thou preparest a table before me in the presence of mine enemies." They may look on if they like; they may grin, they may wish they could devour, but they cannot sit down at the table, and they cannot prevent me from sitting down at it. Let them blow their trumpets, let them fire their guns: "Thou preparest a table before me in the presence of mine enemies." It is the very acme of security and repose that is here described. I know of no expression, not even that of lying down in green pastures, that is more full of restfulness than this: "Thou preparest table before me in the presence of mine enemies."

Verse 5. *Thou anointest my head with oil;*

At some feasts, they poured perfumed unguents on the heads of the guests, so God will leave out nothing that is for the joy and comfort of his people. "Thou anointest my head with oil." You shall have delicacies as well as necessaries; you shall have joy as well as safety; you shall be prepared for service as well as preserved from destruction.

Verse 5. *My cup runneth over.*

I have not only what I wish, but I have more; not only all I can hold, but something to spare: "My cup runneth over." If this is the case with your cup, dear friend, let it run over in thankful joy, and if you have more of this world's substance than you need, ask the poor and needy to come and catch that which flows over.

Verse 6. *Surely*

This is another of the psalmist's inferences, and a very sure one. He does not say, "Peradventure," but, "Surely."

Verse 6. *Goodness and mercy shall follow me all the days of my life:*

Here is a prince of the blood royal of heaven attended by two body guards, — goodness and mercy, — which keep close behind him. These are the grooms that ride on the horses of salvation: "Surely goodness and mercy shall follow me." "Goodness" — to provide for me; "mercy" — to blot out my sin. "Goodness and mercy shall follow me,"-not only now and then, but, "all the days of my life." When I get gray-headed and feeble, and have to lean heavily upon my staff, these twin angels shall be close behind to bear me up, and bear me through.

Verse 6. *And I will dwell in the house of the LORD for ever.*

Even while I am here in this world, I will be "No more a stranger or a guest but like a child at home," dwelling with God; and by-and-by, in the fullest sense, "I will dwell in the house of the Lord for ever." I always compare this Psalm to a lark. It begins on the ground among the sheep, but up it goes till you may hear its blessed notes echoing among the stars: "I will dwell in the house of the Lord for ever." It has its nest in the grass of the green pastures; but it flies up like the strains of sweetest music rising even to the skies: "I will dwell in the house of the Lord for ever." God grant that this may be the portion of every one of us, for his great name's sake! Amen.

APPENDIX 2

"My Father's House" Heaven

BY H. RONDEL RUMBURG

This title comes from the words of our Lord Jesus Christ in John's Gospel chapter 14. "My Father's house" is the Lord Jesus' way of introducing the subject of heaven. The Father's house should be our desired destination once our lost estate has been settled and Christ Jesus is our Salvation. Yes, when the time of our departure comes our prospects arc gloriously bright if we are headed to the Father's house.

Jesus' words, as recorded by John, are glorious: "Let not your heart be troubled: ye believe in God, believe also in me. In my Father's house are many mansions: if *it were* not *so,* I would have told you. I go to prepare a place for you. And if I go and prepare a place for you, I will come again, and receive you unto myself; that where I am, *there* ye may be also.... Peace I leave with you, my peace I give unto you: not as the world giveth, give I unto you. Let not your heart be troubled, neither let it be afraid" (John 14:1-3, 27). This passage is called Jesus' *Farewell Discourse* to His disciples. Yes, some have called it Jesus' swan song.

An army officer approached a wounded soldier on the battlefield. The man lay dying. The officer asked, "Can I do anything for you?" "Nothing—nothing, thank you." "Shall I go and get you a little water?" "No, thank you; I am dying." "Isn't there anything I can do? Cannot I sit down and write a letter to your friends?" "I have no friends you can write to. There is one thing I would be much obliged to you for. In my haversack, yonder, you will find a Testament. Will you open it? Will you be so good as to turn to the fourteenth chapter of John?—and near the end you will find a verse that begins with the word 'Peace.'" The officer turned to the fourteenth of John, and read, *"Peace I leave with you, my peace I give unto you:* not as the world giveth, give I unto you. Let not your heart be troubled, neither let it be afraid." "Thank you, sir," said the dying soldier, "thank you, sir. I have that peace—I am going to that Saviour." In a few moments more the glorified spirit left his poor wounded frame and soared away upwards to the hand of infinite love, which, like the hand of Noah reaching out from the ark to receive the dove, so our Lord receives His own to glory.

Please consider the following from *Hymns New and Old* by D. B. Towner:

> Jesus is mine and I am His,
>   I'll share with Him in Glory;
> There I shall wear a crown of bliss,
>   So says the gospel story.
>
> Over the land and o'er the sea,
>   And o'er the host of heaven;
> The Lord shall reign, and unto me
>   A crown with Him be given.
>
> Oh, what a day of victory
>   When free from toil and sorrow,
> No more despised and poor I'll be,
>   My crown may come to-morrow.
>
> When it will come, oh, no one knows,
>   But day by day it's nearing,
> With crowns of joy and life for those
>   Who love the Lord's appearing.

Glory to God! I soon shall see
The King of kings descending,
And take the crown prepared for me,
In glory never ending.

Jesus' hour had come that He would leave this world via the cross and go back to his Father (John 13:1). Jesus was departing. What would He do after His departure? He would be an intercessor and pray for the Father to "give ... another Comforter" (John 14:16, 26), who is the Holy Spirit. However, in the context of the believer He was going "to prepare a place for you" (John 14:1). This was His promise.

When Jesus was troubled in spirit He explained to His disciples, "Verily, verily, (or truly, truly) I say unto you, that one of you shall betray me" (John 13:21). Peter, who declared that he would die for Jesus, heard the words, "Verily, verily, I say unto thee, The cock shall not crow, till thou hast denied me thrice" (John 13:38). Imagine what must have been on the minds of the disciples as they heard of Jesus being betrayed and denied. They had been brought face to face with the issue that their Lord's time of departure from their presence and this earth had come.

Then in John 14 Jesus began to console and comfort His own as a result of the announcement of His departure. The Lord Jesus made a glorious revelation as the curtain that separates this world from the next was lifted. Actually in this text that curtain was lifted higher than anywhere else in Scripture.

Just think, our Lord on the night of His soul suffering preceding His substitutionary sacrifice for our sins on the cross commanded His disciples to stop being troubled of heart (John 14:1). Yes, there is the command regarding heart trouble and faith in Christ (14:1), then there is the description of the Father's house where a special place is being prepared by Jesus for the believer (14:2), and finally there is the promised return (14:3). A dying scholar uttered the following words after the words of John 14 were read to him, "Inexhaustible, inexhaustible!" Yes, the words of our eternal Lord and Saviour Jesus Christ are "inexhaustible!"

The three verses ... are rich in precious truth. For (twenty) centuries they have been peculiarly dear to Christ's believing servants in every part of the world. Many are the sick rooms which they have lightened! Many are the dying hearts which they have cheered! [J. C. Ryle]

In this passage there is [1] a great commandment (14:1), and [2] the glorious explanation (14:2), and [3] the precious promise (14:3) that the Lord Jesus gives in these verses.

A GREAT COMMANDMENT THAT JESUS GAVE

What is this great commandment that Jesus gave? "Let not your heart be troubled: ye believe in God, believe also in me" (John 14:1). Consider the *first phrase*, "Let not your heart be troubled" or "Stop being so agitated" or "You can stop being agitated now" or "Don't begin to be troubled anymore." The heart is not to be "troubled or agitated." Jesus had personally experienced a "troubled or agitated" heart, for example when Lazarus died, and "When Jesus therefore saw her [Mary] weeping, and the Jews also weeping which came with her, he groaned in the spirit, and was troubled' (John 11:33). The hearts of Jesus' disciples were troubled or agitated—that is they were agitated like a storm tossed sea which dislodges the debris that had been settled on the floor of the sea. These believers had misgivings, questions, disruptive thoughts, etc. cast about in their minds and hearts at the news.

> The hearts of the disciples were filled with a medley of emotions. They were *sad* because of the gloomy prospect of Christ's departure; *ashamed* because of their own demonstrated selfishness and pride; *perplexed* because of the prediction that one of their own number would betray the Master, that another would deny him, and that all would be ensnarled because of him; and finally, they were *wavering* in their faith, probably thinking: "How can one who is about to be betrayed be the Messiah?" Yet, at the same time, they love this Master. They hope against hope. All this is implied in the words, "Let not your hearts any longer be troubled." [William Hendriksen]

This of course is not referring to the physical heart, but it is referring to the seat of spiritual life and center of faith—"For with the heart man believeth unto righteousness; and with the mouth confession is made unto salvation" (Rom. 10:10). Remember Jesus' words, "Thou shalt love the Lord thy God with all thy heart, and with all thy soul, and with all thy mind" (Matt. 22:37). One has called this section of the verse, Jesus' precious remedy against an old disease of spiritual heart trouble.

Consider the *second phrase*, "ye believe in God, believe also in me."[3] We are doubly commanded to stop being

_____

3 "So translated as present active indicative plural second person and present active imperative of πιστευω. The form is the same. Both may be indicative (ye believe ... and ye believe), both may be imperative (believe ... and believe or believe also), the first may be indicative (ye believe) and the second imperative (believe also), the first may be

agitated at heart and instead believe in God and Christ Jesus. The phrase could be translated, "you [need to] keep on believing in God and in me," said Jesus; and this in view of the future blessings that I am going to prepare for you.

The spirit of agitation arose from a lack of faith in what God had said through His prophets concerning Jesus sufferings and the glory that should follow. God had declared in plain terms that Jesus would be despised and rejected of men, and that He would be wounded for our transgressions and bruised for our iniquities. Since God the Father revealed this we need to believe it. Then Jesus said, "believe also in me" for I have warned you about what you should expect. I have told you of My sufferings and death which are coming. Now you need to just trust me.

THE GLORIOUS EXPLANATION JESUS GAVE

The commandment that Jesus gave them regarding their agitated hearts and the necessity to trust God the Father and Himself with the issues of life and eternity is given. There may be earthly agitation of heart but one who reposes in the grace of God in Christ has the prospects of "the Father's house." The believers are strangers and pilgrims on the earth. Why is that true? They are strangers because they are far from home, but they are pilgrims because they are headed home. There are a number of ways heaven is identified: [1] heaven is called a "country" which expresses its vastness (Luke 19:12; Heb. 11:16), [2] heaven is called a "city" which explains it multitude of inhabitants (Heb. 11:10; Rev. 21), [3] heaven is called a "kingdom" which indicates the orderly rule of its King (2 Pet. 1:11), [4]

---

imperative (keep on believing) and the second indicative (and ye do believe, this less likely)." A. T. Robertson heaven is called "paradise" because it is filled with delight (Luke 23:43; Rev. 2:7), and [5] here in our text it is called "the Father's house" which reveals its permanence, perfection, protection, etc.

They had been discouraged because Jesus was going away, but now Jesus encourages them by revealing what He will be doing in His absence. What was that explanation Jesus gave? "In my father's house are many mansions: if it were not so, I would have told you. I go to prepare a place for you" (John 14:2). Thus Jesus encourages them with a declaration of and introduction to His Father's house and what it is like. So there is [1] a place of reunion—in My Father's house, [2] a permanent abiding place—many mansions in the Father's house, [3] an assured place—I would tell you if it were not so, and [4] a prepared place—I go to prepare your place.

First, heaven is a place of reunion—"in my Father's house." Jesus is about to return to the Father from whence He came so He has personal knowledge of His Father's house. The Father's house is a permanent place where the Son of God reunites with His Father. Heaven is Jesus' home and thus because of His atonement will be ours.

A few weeks after the Battle of Fredericksburg (December 13, 1862), about 100,000 Federal soldiers and 70,000 Confederates were camped on opposite sides of the Rappahannock River in Virginia. The battle had been one of the bloodiest of the war. More than 12,000 Federals had been killed or wounded; Confederate losses numbered about 5,000. The two sides were still licking their wounds.

It was customary in the camp at twilight for the regimental bands on each side of the river to began their evening concerts. This was especially true when they were bivouacked close together, as they were on that night. The opposing bands would sometimes play at the same time, trying to drown each other out. On other occasions they took turns. Often the bands waged a musical contest, each playing their own patriotic tunes with as much enthusiasm as they could muster, making many twilight concerts veritable "battles with their band instruments."

As the evening concerts were being brought to a conclusion, the music typically became more heart searching and tender. On one particular night, a Federal band was especially good in its rendition of the War's favorite tune "Home, Sweet Home." The slow, plaintive notes floated like feathers through the air, gently nestling into homesick hearts. Night was the time when men wrote home to their mothers and sweethearts, or held their devotions to the Lord. The soothing notes that night sent the heartfelt words through their minds:

Mid pleasures and palaces though we may roam,
Be it ever so humble there's no place like home!
A charm from the skies seems to hallow us there,
Which, seek through the world,
is ne'er met with elsewhere:
Home! Home! Sweet, sweet Home!
There's no place like Home!
There's no place like Home!

Almost as soon as the Union band began playing "Home, Sweet Home," the Confederate band took it up. One after another, every regimental band in both armies joined together. Everyone stopped what they had been doing. Pens and pencils were put down; books were closed; games were stopped; attentions changed. There wasn't a sound, except for the music.

Then, in the words of Frank Mixson, a private in the 1st South Carolina Volunteers, "Everyone went crazy." Mixson had never witnessed anything like it before. Both sides began cheering, became animated and began throwing their hats into the air. Mixson said the wild cheering that followed the song's lingering notes was confounding. Had there not been a river between them, he reflected, the two armies would have met face to face, shaken hands, and ended the war on the spot.

Fredericksburg wasn't the only time "Home, Sweet Home" made Confederates and Federals forget they were enemies. In the summer of 1864, the Confederates under Maj. Gen. Jubal Early were about to confront Maj. Gen. Phil Sheridan's Federals near Winchester and Martinsburg. Their picket lines were only a few feet apart in some places. As night descended, the pickets began talking to one another. Both sides were exhausted. One of the picket officers called over to the other that he would agree not to fire on their pickets, if the other side would do likewise. This would enable both sides to get a good night's rest. That bargain was rapidly resolved. Even though the pickets desperately needed to sleep, they could not turn in without their evening's musical interlude. The Confederate pickets began singing some of their favorite songs. Then it was the Federals turn to be on stage. After a while, the sentries on either side lined up and sang "Home, Sweet Home" and went happily to sleep.

There is a home that has prospects extremely sweet to the child of God and that home is heaven. What stands between the believer and home? The last river to be crossed before reaching our eternal home or the Father's house is death. This was the river "Stonewall" Jackson spoke of in his death.

Second, heaven is a permanent abiding place—for there "are many mansions or places in which to abide" in the Father's house. There are mansions for all the redeemed to eternally inhabit. Jesus is saying that the Father's house has plenty of room for all believers. Jesus came to fulfill all righteousness and the Spirit came to regenerate all the elect with the result that these will inhabit the Father's house. Paul wrote, "For we know that if our earthly house of this tabernacle were dissolved, we have a building of God, an house not made with hands, eternal in the heavens" (2 Cor. 5:1).

Third, heaven is an assured place—I would tell you if it were not so, declared the Lord. "If it were not so, I would have told you." The point of our Lord here is that he would tell us at once and would not deceive us if this were not true. If there was no room for the redeemed in the Father's house the Lord Jesus would have told us. He is never a deceiver. "To this end was I born (that is to be King)" He said, "and for this cause came I into the world, that I should bear witness unto the truth" (John 18:37). The *Geneva Bible* has the following note, "That is, if it were not as I am telling you, that is, unless there was room enough not only for me, but also for you in my Father's house, I would not deceive you in this way with a vain hope, but I would have plainly told you so." Jesus is saying that He did not conceal any truth. If there was any doubt about heaven He would have told you precisely as He revealed other things to you.

Four, heaven is a prepared place—I go to prepare your place. "I go to prepare a place for you." Again the comfort zone is increased with this last phrase. While away from them Jesus said He was getting a dwelling place in heaven prepared or ready. What was Jesus doing? He was obtaining the right for us to be in the Father's house.

He has 'prepared' for us a place there by entering Heaven as our Representative and taking possession of it on behalf of His people. As our Forerunner He marched in, leading captivity captive, and there planted His banner in the land of glory. He has 'prepared' for us a place there by entering the 'holy of holies' on high as our great High Priest, carrying our names in with Him. Christ would do all that was necessary to secure for His people a welcome and a permanent place in Heaven. Beyond this we cannot go with any degree of certainty. The fact that Christ has promised to 'prepare a place' for us—which repudiates the vague and visionary ideas of those who would reduce Heaven to an intangible nebula—guarantee that it will far surpass anything down here. [A. W. Pink]

THE PRECIOUS PROMISE THAT JESUS MADE

Here is another encouragement to the Lord's people. The promise was "And if I go and prepare a place for you, I will come again, and receive you unto myself; that where I am, there ye may be also" (John 14:3). The verse has been literally translated, "And when I go and prepare a place for you, I come again and will take you to be face to face with me, in order that where I am you may be also" [Hendriksen]. "If I go and I am going" or "when I go" or "seeing I am going" is the sense of this part of the verse. Thus the reason for the departure became the surety of the

205

return. Jesus' going is to "prepare a place for you." Then He declared, "I will come again." So Jesus' going and coming back are certain. Also, the going insures the return. "And receive you unto myself" is the purpose of the return. The return is a mission whereby our Lord will get us and take us to His Father's house. "That is where I am," Jesus said, "there ye may be also." Thus "where I am" said Jesus, which is in the Father's house, "there you may be also" or you will be with Me in the Father's house. The Lord Jesus gives such certainty to the redeemed regarding the place of their eternal abode. Thus we are a prepared people for a prepared place.

CONCLUSION

Thus Jesus said you know where I am going and you know the way (John 14:4). Thomas said, Lord we do not know where you are going so how can we know the way (John 14:5)? Then it was that Jesus said, "I am the way, the truth, and the life; no one comes to the Father in heaven but through Me" (John 14:6).

"Stonewall" Jackson as he entered the last days of his life because of his wounding said:

> It has been a precious experience to me that I was brought face to face with death, and found all was well, I then learned an important lesson: that one who has been the subject of converting grace and is the child of God can, in the midst of the severest sufferings, fix his thoughts upon God and heavenly things, and derive great comfort and peace; but that one who had never made his peace with God would be unable to control his mind, under such sufferings, so as to understand

properly the way of salvation, and repent and believe on Christ. I felt that if I had neglected the salvation of my soul before, it would have been too late then.[4]

What if you were brought face to face with death? Would you find that all was well with your soul? Only if you had experienced saving grace through the atoning work of Christ. Remember those words of Jackson, "I felt that if I had neglected the salvation of my soul before, it would have been too late then."

Consider the words of a dying soldier, "Where else but in Jesus can a poor sinner trust?" Then as the redeemed soldier passed from this life he looked up to heaven uttering, "Heaven is so sweet to me."[5]

---

[4] J. William Jones, *Christ in the Camp*, 98
[5] Jones, 173.

APPENDIX 3

The Revelation of Heaven: The New Heaven and New Earth

PASTOR H. RONDEL RUMBURG

Revelation 21 & 22

INTRODUCTION

"Heaven" does not mean the same thing to all who declare themselves to be Christians. Many think of it in terms of their own utopian dreams coming to fruition. Others contemplate it as a place where they can do their own thing and have their way. Some think of heaven as a materialistic paradise. However, what does the Lord God Almighty reveal about heaven? This is where the truth about heaven is revealed. The child of God wants to know and thus this becomes an important subject to study. Although as already intimated there are probably more misconceptions about heaven than any other place. Some grow weary of this world and long for something better and begin to look beyond this realm. There are those who believe that when you die you cease to exist, so they do not look beyond this life. Then there are those so occupied with this world that they never give heaven a real consideration.

What do you think of when you consider heaven? The answer to that question is quite varied in our time. If you talk to most people they think they are going to heaven some way or other. Their distorted idea of God is such that they believe the Lord to be their God must take everyone into His presence. Pseudo preachers in our day try to "preach everyone into heaven" which, if they could do so, would insure that heaven would literally became a hell! Universalists teach that everyone is going to heaven, which is a contradiction of the teaching of the Lord Jesus Christ and the eternal Word of God. But the old negro spiritual had it right, "Eberybody talkin' 'bout heaben ain't a goin there."

How many falsely envision heaven as a state of weightlessness whereby they float on misty clouds strumming on a harp becoming angels or at least very similar? Some envision a place which is gaudy and has a circus like atmosphere where all lusts are met. There everything glitters and appeals to the greedy fallen nature of mankind.

Heaven is the place where almost everyone plans to go but most expect to get there without any preparation. There is a feeling that somehow they will mysteriously go there regardless of their wickedness because God, who is perceived to be in the image of father time, loves everyone so much He would never send anyone to hell. Truly the words of the Lord Jesus Christ and the Word of God will expel any such idea.

The child of God, because of the redemption in Christ Jesus, has more Biblical expectations. For a good example a few generations ago Harry Rimmer a Biblical scholar wrote a letter to radio preacher Charles E. Fuller just prior to his death. Fuller's subject, "Heaven," had been advertised for the following Sunday. Rimmer wrote,

> Next Sunday you are to talk about Heaven. I am interested in that land because I have held a clear title to a bit of property there for over 50 years. I did not buy it. It was given to me without money and without

price; but the Donor purchased it for me at tremendous sacrifice.

I am not holding it for speculation. It is not a vacant lot. For more than half a century ... the greatest Architect of the Universe has been building a home for me, which will never need remodeling or repairs because it will suit me perfectly, individually, and will never grow old.

Termites can never undermine its foundation for it rests upon the Rock of Ages. Fire cannot destroy it. Floods cannot wash it away. No lock or bolts will ever be placed upon the doors, for no vicious person can ever enter that land, where my dwelling stands, now almost completed and almost ready for me to enter in and abide in peace eternally without fear of being ejected.

There is a valley of deep shadow between this place where I live, and that to which I shall journey in a very short time. I cannot reach my home in that city without passing through this valley. But I am not afraid because the best Friend I ever had went through the same valley long, long ago and drove away all its gloom. He stuck with me through thick and thin since we first became acquainted 55 years ago, and I hold His promise in printed form, never to forsake me or leave me alone. He will be with me as I walk through the valley of the shadow, and I shall not lose my way when He is with me.

I hope to hear your sermon on "Heaven" next Sunday, but I have no assurance I shall be able to do so. My ticket to Heaven has no date marked for the journey, no return coupon and no permit for baggage. Yes, I am ready to go and I may not be here while you are talking next Sunday evening, but I will meet you there some day.

Harry Rimmer

How can a person know what heaven is really like? The great Southern scholar and Baptist preacher John L. Dagg explained,

The light of revelation brings the glories of the distant land before the eyes of our faith; and in the spiritual enjoyment which we are made to experience, even in this land of exile, we have an earnest and foretaste of heavenly joy. These drops of heaven sent down to worms below, unite with the descriptions found in God's holy word, to give such ideas of heaven as it is possible for us to form; but at best, we know only in part.[6]

What kind of impact should a true view of heaven have on the believer? The prospects of eternity with the Triune God should make an impact on us. One has explained,

Christian Hope takes the earth in its arms and goes to the window of the future, and looks out with glorious expectation. When all its changing has come to an end, and its last condition has been crystallized, it hangs out the charming vision of a New Earth, populated with happy individuals, enjoying a righteous and blessed society for evermore.[7]

B. H. Carroll the Baptist pastor and founder of Southwestern Theological Seminary made an excellent

---

[6] J. L. Dagg, *A Manual of Theology*, 358
[7] Robert Alexander Webb, *The Christian's Hope*, 82

observation noting the impact that the prospects of heaven should have on us.

> I want to say, as impressively as I know how to say it, that the reason Christian people are no happier than they are, the reason they have so little power, is that they have such a misty conception of heaven, of the world to come. And whatsoever is misty, is painful. It is only those who, with a clear understanding of God's word as to the outcome of human life, those who by faith see eternal things, and feel the powers of the world to come, who can make any lasting impression for good in this world.[8]

The last two chapters in the Bible include the final vision given to John the Divine, and the subject depicted enters the eternal as well as the consummation of the kingdom of God. The redeemed of the Lord will come to dwell eternally upon the new earth. There is a transformation of all things so that they are new to match the needs of those with new births and new natures. Man brought a curse upon the earth and it must be made remade. Hengstenberg reminds us,

> Everything is now prepared for the entrance of the last phase of the Kingdom of God; for the foundation of the new earth in which righteousness dwells; for the erection upon it of the Kingdom of glory; for the solemnization of the marriage of the Lamb, to the threshold of which we were brought by the song of praise in (Revelation) Chapter 19:6-8. This sacred closing history is the subject of the present group of

---

[8] B. H. Carroll, *An Interpretation of the English Bible: Revelation*, 276

visions. A church which has such a hope will not faint under tribulations. She beholds the end and is comforted.[9]

As we come to consider the new heaven and new earth (Chapter 21), what a contrast this is with the last words of Chapter 20, "And death and hell were cast into the lake of fire. This is the second death. And whosoever was not found written in the book of life was cast into the lake of fire" (vv. 14-15). What encouragement the believer finds in the prospects of the New Heaven, New Earth and New Jerusalem. Truly the Lord will *"make all things new"* (21:5). The prospects could not be brighter following the transformation (Acts 3:19-21). Eternal glory beams afar.

Interestingly the first book in the Bible and the last book in the Bible have significant connections. As one of the Lord's servants has explained it,

> Scripture resembles a flower. We find the seed in Genesis, the growing plant in the books which follow, the fully developed and beautiful flower in the Apocalypse. Observe the following parallel:
>
> Genesis tells us that God created heaven and earth. Revelation describes the *new* heaven and earth, 21:1.
>
> In Genesis the luminaries are called into being: sun, moon, stars. In Revelation we read: "And the city has no need of the sun, nor of the moon, to shine in it; for the glory of God lightened it, and its lamp is the Lamb."
>
> Genesis describes a Paradise which was Lost. Revelation pictures a Paradise Restored, Rev. 2:7; 22:2.

---

[9] Philip Mauro, *Of Things Which Soon Must Come to Pass*, 528

Genesis describes the cunning and power of the devil. The Apocalypse tells us that the devil was bound and was hurled into the lake of fire and brimstone.

Genesis pictures that awful scene: man fleeing away from God and hiding himself from the presence of the Almighty. Revelation shows us the most wonderful and intimate communion between God and redeemed man: "Behold, the tabernacle of God is with men, and he shall tabernacle with them, etc."

Finally, whereas Genesis shows us the tree of life, with an angel to keep the way of the tree of life, "lest man put forth his hand and take of its fruit," the Apocalypse restores to man his right to have access to it: "that they may have the right to come to the tree of life," Rev. 22:14.[10]

In these last two chapters of the book of Revelation we have the description of the final heavenly state of the glorified saints of God. The new habitation of the new creation in Christ is on the new earth where the new Jerusalem will be located after being let down out of heaven.

"Him that overcometh will I make a pillar in the temple of my God, and he shall go no more out: and I will write upon him the name of my God, and the name of the city of my God, [which is] new Jerusalem, which cometh down out of heaven from my God: and [I will write upon him] my new name" (Rev. 3:12). Here is a promise to *"him that overcometh"* and the word is an absolute. Here our Saviour promises a glorious reward to the victorious believer, in two things: *"a pillar"* which pictures something fixed and stable,

---

[10] W. Hendriksen, *More Than Conquerors*, 236 f.

first, he shall be *a monumental pillar in the temple of God*; not a pillar to support the temple (heaven needs no such props), but a monument of the free and powerful grace of God, a monument that shall never be defaced nor removed, as many stately pillars erected in honor to the Roman emperors and generals have been. *Second,* on this monumental pillar there shall be an honorable inscription: [1.] *The name of my God,* in whose cause he engaged, whom he served, and for whom he suffered in this warfare; and *the name of the city of my God, which is the new Jerusalem,* which came down from heaven. On this pillar shall be recorded all the services the believer did for the body of Christ, how he asserted her rights, enlarged her borders, maintained her purity and honor. And then another part of the inscription is, [2.] *Mine own new name* which at present is an incommunicable name known only to the Lord. Christ himself will receive a new name along with all else in the future world. That name which was received from His Father in His exaltation (Eph. 1:20; Phil. 2:9).

I. JOHN'S WITNESS OF HEAVEN.

Consider: what he saw (21:1-2) and what he heard (vv. 3-4).

A. What John Saw (vv. 1-2). John bears witness to three new things that he saw. The *"new"* is in contrast to the *"old."* This has to do with John's witness which is described when he wrote, *"I saw."* The book of *Revelation* is "to shew unto His servants things which must shortly (in God's timetable) come to pass; and He sent and signified it by His angel unto His servant John" (Rev. 1:1, 2). John is used as a servant of God to write these things for our benefit. We can truly say that the purpose of a portion of the book of the Revelation is being brought to pass in our text as John tells us what he saw.

1. John saw a new heaven and a new earth as the old was removed—"And I saw a new heaven and a new earth: for the first heaven and the first earth were passed away; and there was no more sea" (v. 1). Those with the new birth receive the revelation of *"a new heaven and a new earth."* John Trapp gave this explanation, "New for form and state, but the same as before for matter and substance ... and as whoso is in Christ is a new creature." The passage deals with the future state of the church in heaven after the last judgment (21:1-22:5). The entire world is changed for the future habitation of the Lord's people. There are two words in the New Testament translated *"new,"* but there is a difference between them. *One* contemplates the object spoken of under the aspect of something that has been recently brought into existence; *the other* means a fresh aspect given to what had previously existed but has been worn out. The latter word is employed here of the renovation of the old. The word is used also in the phrases a *"new garment"* (Luke 5:36) that is, a garment not threadbare, like an old one; *"new wine-skins"* (Luke 5:37 ff.) that is, skins not shriveled and dried; a *"new tomb"* (Matt. 27:60) that is, not one recently hewn out of the rock, but one which had never been used as the last resting-place of the dead. The fact, therefore, that the heavens and the earth here spoken of are *"new,"* does not imply that they are now for the first time brought into being. They may be the old heavens and the old earth; but they have a new aspect, a new character, adapted to a new end.[11] "The creation of a new heaven and a new earth began with the resurrection,

---

[11] *Expositors Bible*

with Christ the first-fruits of the new humanity and the new creation. The new creation involves the *'shaking'* and recreating of the old world. The first *'shaking'* of the earth took place at Sinai, when the holiness of God in His law was death to the world's sin and rebellion. The second and last shaking began with the resurrection: 'yet once more, I *shake* not the earth only but also heaven' (Heb. 12:26)."[12] The fulfillment of this promise unfolds in John's vision of the New Jerusalem coming down out of heaven to the new earth. The Bible always places redeemed man on a redeemed earth and not in an ethereal realm removed from earthly or earthlike existence. [1] The new heaven will replace the old one. There are three heavens mentioned in the Bible: [a] the atmospheric heaven that engulfs the earth, [b] the starry heavens just outside the earthly atmosphere, and [c] the heaven of heavens where God dwells (also called the third heaven—2 Cor. 12:2). The heavens declare the glory of God. [2] The new earth replaces the old earth. Remember how sin came through man into the garden bringing disaster. After sin death, disease, thorns, thistles, pestilence, bloodshed, and many other problems came as a result, but with the new earth the groaning and travailing stopped. Yes, there was groaning as a result of the fall and its repercussions (Rom. 8:19-22; Matt. 13:41 f.). Remember the flood in Noah's day did not annihilate the earth, but it did change it and it was called a new earth. With the fiery purging the earth is not thereby annihilated. The next major event for the earth itself is reconstructive surgery, so to speak, for there is a fire for purification (Rev. 6:13, 14; 2 Pet. 3:7-14). We have the expectations of a new universe. "In our imagination let us try to see this new universe. The very

---

[12] R. J. Rushdoony

foundations of the earth have been subjected to the purifying fire. Every stain of sin, every scar of wrong, every trace of death, has been removed. Out of the great conflagration a new universe has been born. The word used in the original implies that it was a *'new'* but not an *'other'* world. It is the same heaven and earth, but gloriously rejuvenated: no weeds, thorns, thistles, etc. (Gen. 3:18). Nature comes to its own: all of its potentialities, dormant so long, are now fully realized. The *'old'* order has vanished. The universe in which the dragon, the beast, the false prophet, and the harlot were carrying out their program of iniquity has vanished. The sea, as we now know it, is no more.... Remember: the **same** universe, but renewed!"[13] The old world is gone. "For the first heaven and the first earth were passed away or disappeared." The old sin scarred heaven and earth are completely renovated. [3] *"There was no more sea."* There was a new heaven and earth but not a new sea. The sea symbolizes the nations in their former conflict and unrest (Rev. 13:1-7; 17:1, 15). Isaiah compares the wicked to the tossing of the restless sea (Isa. 57:20-21). The sea will have already given up its dead (Rev. 20:13). There will be no turbulence or distress in the new heaven and earth. Seas at one time divided nations, this purports that all barriers are removed. "The redeemed race will be one, no longer many, and no longer needing to be protected against each other's aggression by interposed oceans. The conditions of life will be changed, and that *'highway of nations,'* now used for so many purposes, will be needed no longer."[14] Just as the old earth and heaven

---

13 Hendriksen, 239
14 Justin A. Smith, 287

have literally been dealt with even so there is no need for a literal sea.

2. John saw a New Jerusalem—"And I John saw the holy city, new Jerusalem, coming down from God out of heaven, prepared as a bride adorned for her husband" (v. 2). There is something important to remember, the name *"new Jerusalem"* as used in the book of Revelation is always accompanied by the phrase *"coming down from heaven."* This identifies the origin of the *"new Jerusalem."* [a] Which Jerusalem is John referring to in this passage? This is not the old Jerusalem in Palestine that has been destroyed, but this refers to "the Jerusalem ... coming down from heaven" and "the Jerusalem above" (Gal. 4:26), this is the spiritual Jerusalem; the city consisting of those whose citizenship is in heaven (Phil. 3:20); the true church Jesus bought with His own blood. Jerusalem was the place where God was worshipped, and therefore it became synonymous with the word "church or congregation," which represents the people of God. The word rendered *"above"* means, properly, up above, that which is above; and hence heavenly or celestial; Colossians 3:1 says, "If ye then be risen with Christ, seek those things which are *above*, where Christ sitteth on the right hand of God" and verse 2 continues, "Set your affection on things *above*, not on things on the earth." Jesus declared in John 8:23, "And he said unto them, Ye are from beneath; I am from *above*: ye are of this world; I am not of this world." Jesus did not intend to prepare the earthly Jerusalem for us, but He said "I go [it was out of this world system that He went] to prepare a place for you" (John 14:2). In our present passage it means, the heavenly or celestial Jerusalem. "And I John saw the holy city, new Jerusalem, coming down from God, out of heaven." John continues to bear testimony! "Ye are come unto mount Sion, and unto the city of the living God, the heavenly Jerusalem" (Heb. 12:22). Note: "And unto the city of the living God." This is the city inhabited by the living God—the heavenly Jerusalem. God dwelt symbolically in the literal temple at Jerusalem. In a more literal and glorious sense his abode is in heaven, and to that his people have now come. Hebrews 12:22 continues *"the heavenly Jerusalem."* Heaven is frequently represented as a magnificent city, where God and angels dwell; and the Divine revelation discloses this to Christians as assuredly their final home. Believers can regard themselves already as dwellers in that city, and live and act as if they saw its splendor, and partook of its joy. For it is *"by faith* we understand.*"* Heaven is the city where God dwells (comp. Heb. 11:10, 14-16; 12:28; 13:14; Gal. 4:26; Rev. 3:12; 21:2, 10-27). Christians have not yet *seen* that city with their own eyes, but they may open the eye of faith. Christians may anticipate and contemplate future glories, and act upon the fact that such is their eternal home. Our Lord permits us to live and act *as if* we could see the glorious God whose dwelling is there, and remember we shall be surrounded by the angels and the redeemed. The Bible does represent them as being now actually dwellers in that city, and bound to live and act as if we are in the midst of heavenly splendor (Eph. 1:3). Here *"the heavenly Jerusalem"* is used to denote the church, as being of heavenly origin. [b] What city is this to which John refers when he called it "the holy city?" Of Abraham it was said, "For he looked for a city which hath foundations, whose builder and maker is God" (Heb. 11:10). *"For"* "intimates that a reason is given in these words why Abraham behaved ... as a sojourner on the earth; it was

221

because he knew that his portion did not lie in the things here below, but he looked for things of another nature, which by this means were to be obtained."[15] This verse explains, "For he *looked for* [or expected] a city which hath foundations." Some have been conflicted as to what the apostle was referring. There were people who supposed that Abraham was looking for an earthly Jerusalem, as a permanent dwelling for his posterity in place of his nomadic existence. There is no Biblical evidence that Abraham looked forward to the building of such a city, for God made no such promise to him; and such an interpretation does not seem to fit this passage (Comp. Heb 11:12, 14-16; 12:22; 13:14). "He *looked for a city,*" and this was a heavenly city the eternal abode of God, which God has prepared for all true believers. They have a glorious prospect of something better—"But now they desire a better country, that is an heavenly: wherefore God is not ashamed to be called their God: for He hath prepared for them a city" (Heb. 11:16). Heaven is sometimes referred to as a house (2 Cor. 5:1), a tabernacle (Luke 16:9) and a mansion (John 14:2). Phrases such as: "the city of God," "a city with foundations," "the new Jerusalem," and "the heavenly Jerusalem" in the time of the apostles appear to have acquired a kind of symbolism. They referred to the area—of which Jerusalem, the seat of the worship of God, seem to have been regarded as the emblem. Thus in Hebrews 12:22, the apostle spoke of the *"heavenly Jerusalem,"* and in Hebrews 13:14, he says, "here have we no continuing city, but we seek one to come." In Revelation 21:2, John says that he "saw the holy city, new Jerusalem, coming down from God out of heaven," and proceeded in that chapter and the following to give a most

---

[15] John Owen, *An Exposition of Hebrews*, Vol. 7, 69

beautiful description of it. Even so early as the time of Abraham, it would seem that the future blessedness of the righteous was foretold under the image of a splendid City built on permanent foundations showing stability. It is remarkable that Moses does not mention this as an object of the faith of Abraham, and it is impossible to comprehend the degree of distinctness in view. Abraham *"looked for or expected a city"* where he would eternally rest with the Lord. This is a demonstration of faith in what was not seen as yet (2 Cor. 4:16-18). It is probable that the apostle, in speaking of his faith in particular; a place where the worship of God would be celebrated for ever—a city of which Jerusalem was the most striking representation to the mind of a Jew. It was natural for him to speak of strong piety in this manner wherever it existed, and especially in such a case as that of Abraham, who left his own habitation to wander in a distant land. This fact showed that he regarded himself as a stranger and sojourner; and yet he had a strong expectation of a fixed habitation, and a permanent inheritance. He must, therefore, have looked beyond to the permanent abode of the righteous—the heavenly city. Abraham had an undoubted confidence that the promised land would be given to his posterity, yet, as he did not possess it himself, he must have looked for his own permanent abode and fixed residence in heaven. This passage proves that Abraham had an expectation of future happiness after death. The passage implies that Abraham expected the possession of the Promised Land for his posterity, yet his faith looked beyond this for a permanent home in a future world. This was a city "whose builder and maker is God." Man's efforts do not have a part in this construction, but God was its immediate and direct architect. The apostle here commends the faith of Abraham as eminently strong. [c] Who will inhabit this Jerusalem? "Him that overcometh will I make a pillar in the temple of my God, and he shall go no more out; and I will write upon him the name of my God, and the name of the city of my God, which is new Jerusalem, which cometh down out of heaven from my God: and I will write upon him my new name" (Rev. 3:12). The *"overcomer or conqueror"* [the Greek word here is the one from which we get Nike] will inhabit the *"new Jerusalem."* We are more than conquerors through Christ (Rom. 8:37). The conqueror is established— "I will make a pillar" or give him permanent status. He is made a pillar "in *the temple of my God."* "Therefore are they before the throne of God, and serve him day and night in his temple: and he that sitteth on the throne shall dwell among them" (Rev. 7:15). "But if I tarry long, that thou mayest know how thou oughtest to behave thyself in the house of God, which is the church of the living God, the pillar and ground of the truth" (1 Tim. 3:15). The conqueror "shall go no more out." Here in Revelation 3:12, "no more" is a double negative which demonstrates his fixed position even as a pillar. He has an unchanging position in the perfect presence of God. He will never be dispossessed for he has an eternal inheritance. Ownership is established—"and I will write upon him the name of my God" (Rev. 3:12). He will also write on him "the name of the city of My God, which is new Jerusalem" and this marks the person and the place securing the position of the child of God. The "new Jerusalem, which cometh down out of heaven from My God" and this fixes the place and progression of the New Jerusalem. The establishing of ownership continues—"and I will write upon him My new name." This new name indicated a *new* relation, new hopes and triumphs. [d] The presentation of the new Jerusalem. The holy city, new Jerusalem was "prepared as a bride adorned for her husband" (Rev. 21:2). The bride is "prepared or made ready"—heaven is a prepared place for a prepared people. What perfection in preparation! This bride is *"adorned."* The word here is the one from which we get our word "cosmetics." An adorned bride is one that is brought to the height of her beauty. However, this has reference not to the people of God (19:7) but to the place of their eternal abode. The adornment is given in Revelation 21:11-21.

Some concluding thoughts on the new universe described in Revelation 21 verses 1 and 2. This will be the eternal home of those with eternal life. Living upon the earth is a very natural experience for men. Jesus said, "Blessed are the meek: for they shall inherit the earth" (Matt. 5:5). "For evildoers shall be cut off; But those that wait upon the LORD, they shall inherit the earth.... The righteous shall inherit the land, and dwell therein for ever" (Ps. 37:9, 29).

B. What John Heard (Rev. 21:3-4). John had expressed, by God's imperative, what he saw and now he comes before us to tell us what he heard. "And I heard," said John; in other words his personal testimony of what he heard will be expressed now by Holy Spirit enablement. Here he describes [1] the kind of voice he heard—*"a great voice,"* [2] the origin of the voice—*"out of heaven,"* [3] the sayings of the voice (vv. 3-4).

1. The kind of voice that John heard—*"a great voice."* John said "I heard" a great voice and then he gave his personal witness of the voice. God may speak in a "still small voice" or in "a great voice," but it is His prerogative to know and do this according to His perfect nature along with His perfect timing. There is a phrase repeated in the letters to the seven churches—"He that hath an ear, let him hear what the Spirit saith unto the churches" (Rev. 2:7, 11, 17, etc.). One must have spiritual hearing, and that is what John had, for the Holy Spirit spoke to him. Jesus said of the religious leaders of His day "having ears, (but) you hear not" (Mark 8:18). Why could they not hear while John could hear? "The natural man receiveth not the things of the Spirit of God: for they are foolishness unto him: neither can he know them, because they are spiritually discerned" (1 Cor. 2:14). Unregenerate men cannot understand the voice of God. This voice that John heard was great in its source, in its purpose and in its power. This is the voice of authority. Remember in creation how "God said, Let there be light: and there was light" (Gen. 1:3). This great voice that John heard was a confirmation of the vision that John just mentioned that he saw (Rev. 21:1-2), perhaps this is to prevent a thought that this might be a delusion.

2. The origin of the voice that John heard— *"out of heaven."* What does this mean? This must mean that it originated with God! *"Heaven"* in Scripture is the place of God's permanent abode. It is where He is enthroned. This is the seat of God's government, worship and presence. We know this could not refer to the first heaven because it has passed away (Rev. 21:1), but this is the place where God resides. Therefore God is speaking to John.

3. The sayings of the voice that John heard (vv. 3-4). "What is said here, is applicable to the church of God in this life, yea, to every true believer, whose body is said to be the temple of the Lord, and in whom the Lord dwells, according to the phrase of the Holy Ghost in many places of the New Testament...."[16] In this passage is the message of heaven: it speaks of God's relationship to His people (v. 3), it speaks of God's promise to His people (v. 4), and it speaks of God's faithfulness to His people (vv. 5-6). Here is something God wants us to know: [1] "Behold, the tabernacle of God is with men...." This was the first thing that John heard. The word *"behold"* is used to attract attention to the glorious truths that follow. The word *"behold"* is like a great index finger asking for attention and pointing out truth. [a] Our attention is thus drawn to "the tabernacle of God." When the Lord's people were traveling through the wilderness the sacred tent or tabernacle represented God's presence among His people, but His presence was approachable only through a mediator and a blood sacrifice. The tabernacle had an entrance, a holy place and a holy of holies. Thus God was approachable in the prescribed way. The meaning here must be that God dwells with His redeemed ones for He has a prepared residence in their midst. In this contest *"the tabernacle"* does not refer to a temporary abode, but a permanent one. The Greek word here translated *"the tabernacle"* is a word closely related to the Hebrew *"Shekinah."* The Greek word used here is the word used to translate Shekinah in the Septuagint, and it denotes the glory of God's presence among men. In John 1:14 we are told that "the Word was made flesh, and *dwelt or tabernacled* among us." Jesus the Christ the Son of God has tabernacled on the earth for "God was with us." [b] Note that the text goes on to say the tabernacle of God is *"with men."* Remember what God the Father said through His messenger about His Son who came in the flesh, "they shall call His name Emmanuel,

---

[16] Matthew Poole

which being interpreted is, God with us" (Matt. 1:23). The Lord Jesus was with us in grace and ultimately in glory.

A Vision of the Kingdom of Christ among Men
(Revelation 21:1-4)

Lo, what a glorious sight appears
 To our believing eyes!
The earth and sea are passed away,
 And the old rolling skies.

From the third heaven where God resides,
 That holy, happy place,
The New Jerusalem comes down
 Adorn'd with shining grace.

Attending angels shout for joy,
 The bright armies sing,
'Mortals, behold the sacred seat
 of your descending King.

The God of glory down to men
 Removes his blest abode,
Men the dear objects of his grace,
 And he the loving God.

His own soft hand shall wipe the tears
 From every weeping eye,
And pains and groans, and griefs, and fears
 And death itself shall die.'

How long dear Saviour, O how long,
 Shall this bright hour delay!
Fly swifter round, ye wheels of time,
 And bring the welcome day.

Remember how God historically came among men: God walked in Eden and talked to Adam and Eve, God appeared to the patriarchs of old and spoke to them, God dwelt in darkness in the unseen and innermost part of the tabernacle in the wilderness, God was in Christ in the days of His flesh, God dwells in His Church by His Spirit, but the eternal and unchanging representation is that God will dwell with His redeemed people eternally. John is conveying two thoughts in our text: God is present and God is glorious in his presence. The word of our text is used in the book of Hebrews with reference to heaven (Heb. 8:2; 9:11; see Ps. 61:4 and Rev. 15:5). Another thing God wants his people to know [2] "And He will dwell with them, and they shall be His people" (Rev. 21:3b). "And He will dwell with them." This dwelling was referred to earlier— "Therefore are they before the throne of God, and serve him day and night in his temple: and he that sitteth on the throne shall dwell among them" (Rev. 7:15; see Ez. 37:27; Zech. 2:10; 8:8). Also, as we have noted it refers to the incarnation of Jesus Christ on earth (John 1:14). And it referred, as noted, to the Shekinah Glory of God. God dwells with His people and when He is with us there is light. Even now He dwells in His church through the Holy Spirit. God's dwelling presence with His people was even referred to by Solomon in his dedicatory prayer of the temple (1 Kings 8:12-13; cf. vv. 30, 39, 43; 2 Chron. 6:2). The Greek word for dwell is used in Revelation 7:15; 12:12; 13:6 and 21:3. "And they shall be His people" (Rev. 21:3). *"They"* is emphatic for they are His without doubt, they were elected by God the Father, they were redeemed by God the Son, they were regenerated by God the Spirit, they were effectually called by God the Spirit and now this is made most evident. *"They"* shall literally be *"His peoples."* God's people belong to Him by creation, preservation, redemption, regeneration and glorification. Heaven is heaven because God is there with His people, but hell is what it is because God is not present with those inhabiting that place. John also makes the assertion [3] "And God himself shall be with them" (Rev. 21:3). Again the Immanuel theme is asserted. This relationship speaks of direct and unmarred fellowship between God and His people as a result of redemption. The personal presence of God will now be enjoyed whereas before it would have been destructive, but now they are glorified (Ez. 48:35). Presently we look through a glass darkly, but then face to face (1 Cor. 13:12), now we are God's sons but it does not yet appear what we shall be (1 John 3:2). Then shall we ever be with the Lord (1 Thess. 4:17). Not only is God with us, but God shall *"be their God."* This asserts God's initiative taking grace. Thomas said of the risen Christ, "my Lord, and my God" (John 20:28), and here God says to us that He is our God, and it is on the basis of the covenant of grace. "Happy is that people, that is in such a case: yea, happy is that people, whose God is the LORD" (Ps. 144:15). John Brown of Haddington wrote, "Reading tires me, walking tires me, riding tires me; but were I once with Jesus, fellowship with Him will never tire me. 'So shall we ever be with the Lord.' Oh, that sweet little sentence! 'We shall be forever with the Lord.' Oh, how sweet—forever with the Lord! And that which makes the wonder is this, that it is we that are to enjoy this happiness; we pitiful wretches are to be forever with God our Saviour—God in our nature." John Newton the writer of *Amazing Grace* made a rather startling statement, "When I get to heaven I shall see three wonders there. The *first* wonder will be, to see many people there whom I did not expect to see—the *second* wonder will be to miss many people whom I did expect to see; and the *third* and greatest wonder of all, will be to find myself there." [4] John heard a promise from God (Rev. 21:4). [a] What God promised regarding sorrowful tears (v. 4a), [b] what God promised about death (v. 4b), [c] what God promised regarding pain (v. 4c). Please consider [a] what God promised regarding sorrowful tears—"And God shall wipe away all tears from their eyes" (v. 4a). If the tears are wiped out of the eyes then the cause of those tears must be removed or placated. [i] God wipes every tear *out of* their eyes, [ii] God's act of wiping away tears shows compassion, [iii] God's provision for tears in life is a blessing, [iv] God's allowance of tears in this life characterizes fallen man, and [v] God has a tearless world for the redeemed. Before we consider these points just listen to a comparison from Matthew Poole, "Scarce any of the passages in this verse, taken in the plain, literal sense, are applicable to any state of the church in this life: for though in the thousand years, mentioned Rev. 20:1-3, the state of the church (as it is presumed) will be very happy comparatively to what it ever was before, and free from its enemies' molestations and persecutions; yet I think none hath asserted that in that time no members of it shall die, or be sick, or have any sorrow or pain. There must be a great allowance of figures, if we will apply this to any state of the militant church; but all will be literally true as to the church in heaven." Dr. John Gill described the general cause of tears, "Occasioned by sin, Satan, the hidings of God's face, and afflictive dispensations of Providence...." And we could add joy and rejoicing occasions tears.

[i] God wipes every tear out of their eyes—
"And God shall wipe away all tears from their eyes...." What we need to know is, what does this mean in relation to saved beings. Just think of a tearless existence. As we begin to look at this phrase of Scripture it portends something good to come, and should give us great encouragement for we live in a world containing a great deal of crying. This life is often called "a vale of tears." Robert Browning penned,

> "What is he buzzing in my ears?
> 'Now that I come to die,
> Do I view the world as a vale of tears?'
> Ah, reverend sir, not I!"

Thank God that because of redemption through the Lord Jesus Christ we shall not experience an eternity of "weeping and wailing and gnashing of teeth" (Matt. 8:12). Our eternity will be just the opposite of this condition because God will insert Himself into our situation and make a permanent difference. And what our God does it shall be forever. Yes, God wipes every tear out of their eyes—*"God shall wipe away all tears from their eyes...."* (v. 4a). How often did our mothers wipe away our tears? Their effort was only temporary. Who shall permanently wipe them away—*"And God...."* Previously John recorded, "and God Himself shall be with them, and be their God." *"And God"* who is mentioned in the text is literally *"the God."* What a reminder of invincible deity. The only one who can remedy us of tears is God Himself. To what extent are they wiped away—*"wipe away all tears from their eyes...."* The wonderful process of "wiping away or blotting out" is in our future. "For the Lamb which is in the midst of the throne shall feed them, and shall lead them unto living fountains of

232

waters: and God shall wipe away all tears from their eyes" (Rev. 7:17). Isaiah had spoken of this glorious event, "He will swallow up death in victory; and the Lord GOD will wipe away tears from off all faces; and the rebuke of his people shall he take away from off all the earth: for the LORD hath spoken it" (Isa. 25:8). All the philosophical, sociological and psychological attempts to cure man of his tears have failed. It is only *"the God"* of the Bible who shall permanently succeed. For He alone can remove the very cause of them. Yes, God shall abolish forever the debilitating effects of sin through the work of Christ and at a future point once and for all remove the weeping. Truly this world is "a vale of tears" but there is a world to come that will see the eradication of them. Since there is no more cause for tears, such as death, mourning, crying and pain (as in Rev. 16:10) there is peace and bliss. Tear free eyes means all of the causes of those tears have been once and for all removed. "All tears" or "every single tear" will be removed because they are eradicated by Divine omnipotence.

[ii] God's act of wiping away tears shows compassion toward His redeemed. The fact that there are tears to wipe away indicates the need for God's compassion. Matthew Henry remarked, "God himself, as their tender Father, with his own kind hand, *shall wipe away the tears* of his children; and they would not have been without those tears when God shall come and wipe them away." In this text we are introduced to some of the negative aspects of heaven. The first one in our text regards the abolition of tears, and may be the most productive in consoling the saints. The reason is this world is entered in tears, lived with a mingling of tears and exited in tears. There have been a number of definitions of "man" but

233

perhaps the one that best describes man is "the weeping one." Yes, the tears are exterminated by the permanent removal of their cause. However, those who in this life were never brought to weep in repentance over their sins will never have their tears removed in eternity for eternal death has eternal tears.

[iii] God's provision for tears in life is a blessing. Tears within this "vale of tears" are often useful in diffusing pent up emotions. Thus tears are not always bad. Tears may be a means of giving vent to the heart, which can be very consoling. Thus we "weep with those who weep" (Rom. 12:15). Remember those famous words, "It is better to go to the house of mourning" the Hebrew word refers to the loud wailing customary in that part of the world at the time of burial and for thirty days thereafter, "than to go to the house of feasting: for that is the end of all men; and the living will lay it to his heart. Sorrow is better than laughter: for by the sadness of the countenance the heart is made better. The heart of the wise is in the house of mourning; but the heart of fools is in the house of mirth" (Eccl. 7:2-4). Certainly the point of the Preacher in Ecclesiastes is that the sorrowful tears of mourning are for the ultimate good by sobering the mind and focusing the heart. Laughter does not make the heart eternally better, but the tears of repentance may afford eternal value. Emotions in themselves may be of no value to the soul of man, but the neo-Platonists, stoics and quietists are wrong for they believe that emotion is totally of no value. Just as the soul may be lost even so it, by grace, may be saved, even so the emotions may be purely fleshly or they may be of spiritual use. God in His infinite wisdom provided man with this outlet because the fall would make it very needful. In this world tears can bring some relief. Consider the following example: When a born again loved one dies the Bible does not say we are not to weep, but it does say that we weep not as others who have no hope (1 Thess. 4:13). Our blessed Lord Jesus is recorded as weeping three times in the New Testament: He wept over Jerusalem (Luke 19:41), He wept over Lazarus (John 11:35), and He wept in the garden over sin (Heb. 5:7).

Tears are the expression of the tenderness of heart, the exuberance of joy, the language of sorrow and the symbol of grief. The emotions must be allowed to speak within the guidelines of God (as in 1 Thess. 4:13) or the heart will be crushed by the pressure. This does not necessarily mean that everyone has literal tears, but the expression will be there just the same. However, we must beware of emotionalism, which is a state of acting purely from emotion rather than the directive of Scripture by the Holy Spirit. Sadly some equate emotionalism with the Holy Spirit's work.

Octavious Winslow expressed it this way, "Our emotions seek an outlet; our feelings demand an expression; love yearns to confide, and grief pines to repose. Suppress these emotions of the soul, conceal these feelings of the heart, shroud these thoughts of the mind, chill and petrify these sensibilities of our humanity, and you have gone far effectually to impair, if not entirely to destroy, one of the noblest creations of God—a loving heart, a sensitive spirit, a refined and thoughtful mind.... What a divinely wise and beneficent provision then is tears! What a safety-valve of the soul! What an outlet of the profoundest grief and of the intensest love, and what an inlet of the divinest joy and the sweetest repose!"[17]

[iv] God's allowance of tears in this life characterizes fallen man. "Behold the tears of the oppressed..." (Eccl. 4:1 ff.; 2:10 ff.). Man comes into this life from the womb in tears as a sign of life in Adam. He, in his depravity, goes from tears to tears as long as his life shall last. Man when he dies is attended with tears. Just to think that without Christ he shall spend eternity in weeping and wailing and gnashing of teeth.

Believers need to remember that their tears are not symbols of sorrow and suffering. Winslow asserted, "But tears are not all symbols of woe, or expressions of suffering—unmusical and voiceless. They often come on a divine embassy and speak in the language of heaven. The blessings they scatter from their dewy wings are many and precious. Sanctified by grace, they soften our rugged nature, cool our fevered passions, recall our truant affections, and, detaching our minds from the things that are seen and temporal, they fix them more entirely upon the things that are unseen and eternal."[18] For believers there is an eternal prospect of joy.

[v] God has a tearless world for the redeemed. The tearless abode is insured by God using His power to wipe away all tears. Also, this insures that there will be no further cause of crying. We have considered the important uses of tears in this life, but there are no such uses in the heavenly life to come. Real tears have no place because there would be nothing for them to relieve. The glorified body shall have no weaknesses for it shall be like

---

[17] O. Winslow, *Pisgah Views or Negative Aspects of Heaven*, 130
[18] Winslow, 131

Christ's glorious body. There will be no more tears from Christ for there will be no more dead Lazarus' to weep over. (1) There will be no more tears of repentance in the New Jerusalem. There will be no more sin to sorrow over. Peter will not be in the position to have to sorrow and weep bitterly as before (Matt. 26:75). The Lord Jesus will not behold this New Jerusalem and weep over it as He did the old one (Luke 19:41). Our beds will not be wet with tears as they sometimes are in this world (Ps. 6:6). Paul will no longer serve the Lord with many tears (Acts 20:17-22). Paul ceased not to warn them with tears night and day (Acts 20:31), but no more. Paul wrote the sinful church at Corinth with many tears (2 Cor. 2:4), but this will not happen anymore. Paul will not have to weep over erring saints (Phil. 3:18). There will be no more weeping over lost sinners as now (Ps. 126:5, 6). Tears of repentance are wonderful now for they speak of sin rejected, sin hated, sin forgiven and sin forsaken. But heaven has no need of tears of repentance for there is no sin there. (2) There will be no more tears of suffering in the New Jerusalem. Why? As we shall see later there will be *"no more pain."* Heaven does not, yea, cannot have suffering. What a pain free future. (3) There will be no more tears of affliction in the New Jerusalem. We know our Father never causes us a needless tear. But now when we disobey there must be discipline. Now chastening is a mark of love, "whom the Lord loveth he chasteneth" (Heb. 12:6; Prov. 13:24). Chastening presently does not seem joyous but grievous (Heb. 12:11). Affliction in the present world can be good—"It is good for me that I have been afflicted; that I might learn Thy statutes" (Ps. 119:71). Affliction in this life is corrective for the wayward saint. But heaven has no need for the rod of correction or affliction, for saints are like

Christ there. (4) There will be no more tears of bereavement in the New Jerusalem. There will never be any goodbyes in heaven. No more separation from those we love, no strain to get that last look, no searching the imagination to reconstruct a fading image, no having to bid a fond farewell, no having to hear the last gasp and no having to commit them to the foe of death. Why is that true? There shall not be any death. Faith reaches out its hand beyond the parting and sees the eternal meeting. Remember, death which separates us now will reunite us there with those "who die in the Lord." "Blessed are the dead that die in the Lord" (Rev. 14:13). When you walk to the grave remember the rejoicing in heaven and the prospects of reunion where the tears of bereavement will be wiped out by the pierced hand of Christ. (5) There will be no more tears for an absent Saviour. Remember how Mary wept at Jesus' tomb? There is a longing to be with Christ and heaven will have His eternal presence (Isa. 30:18-19).

CONCLUSION OF *"NO MORE TEARS."*

1) Beware of placing the wrong emphasis on emotion instead of Christ. Religious feeling may exist without real conversion. One may weep at a description of Christ's sufferings (like the women observing Jesus on the way to the cross or like those watching the movies of Jesus' suffering) or one may weep at a description of heaven's happiness without a change of heart, a holy life or a hope of glory.

2) Remember the provision that God has made for tearful saints. For repenting tears there is the blood of Christ Jesus. For suffering tears there is the changeless love of Christ. For sorrowing tears there is the sympathetic

Christ who is touched with the feelings of our infirmities. For afflictive tears there is the Lord who sticks closer than a brother. For bereaving tears there is the promise of no more death in the living Christ.

3) Remember it is only the Lord who can wipe away all tears (Isa. 25:8).

> Oh, for the robes of whiteness!
> > Oh, for the tearless eyes!
> Oh, for the glorious brightness
> > Of the unclouded skies!
>
> Oh, for the no more weeping,
> > Within the land of love—
> The endless joy of keeping
> > The bridal feast above!
>
> Oh, for the bliss of dying,
> > My risen Lord to meet!
> Oh, for the rest of lying
> > Forever at His feet!
>
> Oh, for the hour of seeing,
> > My Saviour face to face!
> The hope of ever being
> > In that sweet meeting-place.
>
> Jesus, Thou King of glory!
> > I soon shall dwell with Thee;
> I soon shall sing the story
> > Of Thy great love to me.
>
> Meanwhile my thoughts shall enter
> > E'en now before thy Throne,
> That all my love may centre
> > In Thee-and thee alone.

YES, "GOD SHALL WIPE AWAY ALL TEARS FROM THEIR EYES."

[5] John heard another promise from God— "and there shall be no more death" (Rev. 21:4). One of the great causes of tears is removed. Are there many now who do not believe in the fact of death? Are there many who would ignore death? Are there many who will escape death? Consider the evil Louis XV (1710-1774), the king of France, who had a great fear of death. He was one of the lewdest and wickedest kings of all Europe. He had a series of mistresses and court favorites who dominated him. Madame de Pompadour dominated him for 20 years, while she dictated state policy and appointed ministers of state. These, so called friends, looted the treasuries of France. Louis foolishly decreed that death was never to be spoken of in his presence. Nothing that reminded him of death in any way was to be spoken in his presence or displayed. He sought to avoid every place, sign or monument that would suggest death. However, the perverted king Louis died of smallpox in 1774. But for the citizen of the New Jerusalem there is no fear of death for it shall be totally annihilated. Presently death is anticipated and greatly dreaded. Death claims every individual as its victim, makes every home a place of mourning sometime, turns the world into a vast cemetery, cuts the fondest of earthly ties, extinguishes the brightest of hopes, and saddens the hardest of hearts.

1) The definition of death. Consider death abstractly, negatively and positively. *Abstractly* death is a calamity filling the mind with uncertainty, the heart with grief and the future with dread. It is a mystery of the unknown. *Negatively* death is not soul sleep because Paul said, to be absent from the body is to be present with the Lord (2 Cor. 5:8). Death is not soul annihilation (Eccl. 12:7). *Positively* there is physical, spiritual and eternal death.

What is death? What is physical death? It is the separation of the soul from the body wherein the body goes back to its original material. Death is a mysterious end, but in reality it ends nothing. Jesus said, "And whosoever liveth and believeth in Me shall never die" (John 11:26). Spiritual death is being dead to God and the blessings of His grace. Jesus came to bring life and light. Eternal death is an unending separation from God in hell. Thankfully there are no graves in heaven.

2) The cause of death. (a) The originating cause of death was sin (Gen. 2:17; Rom. 5:12; 6:23). (b) The necessitating cause of death was mercy. In a world of sin and corruption death is a ministry of mercy (this does not condone mercy killing). Just as pain makes the eyelid blink to protect it from further danger so the possibility of death is a warning to protect and preserve existing life. Would it be a blessing to us if people did not die in this life? Death is the offspring of sin in this world of sinners and a necessity. Suppose a Hitler, a Khrushchev, a Herod, a Son of Sam, etc. never died. Suppose rapists, thieves, sodomites, perverts, swindlers, etc. never died. Death is necessary as long as sin is in the human heart. In the present kind of world death is an ally of peace. The drowning of the world in Noah's day was a way of preserving a remnant. Everlasting life for a world full of sinners would be a curse of damnation for all. This is why man was driven out of the Garden of Eden from access to the tree of life (Gen. 3:24). Death has a mercy and love in it because it terminates perverts, abortionists, oppressors, tyrants, etc. Note the language of Job 3:17, "There the wicked cease from troubling; and there the weary be at rest." One has written, "As long then as there is sin in our world, and suffering the consequence of that sin, death comes a beneficent messenger to relieve the slave in the Dismal Swamp from the oppressive master whose chains can no longer bind him." Considering the condition of this world death is a necessary intruder. In death itself there is an element of mercy. Although death is sure there is a benefit in not knowing when, where and how it will come, which avoids despair.

Consider the following illustration: Frederick William the Third of Prussia made a remarkable experiment. Six persons who had been condemned to death for murder were submitted to a medical experiment at the request of physicians. Three of the persons were put in unchanged beds where cholera patients had died, but they were not told about the patients. Three of the persons were put into perfectly clean beds which had never had any cholera patients in them, but they were told that cholera patients died in them. The results were that the three in the cholera beds did not die, but the three in the clean beds died because they believed death to be imminent and the suspense crushed the life out of them.

3) The destruction of death. "And there shall be no more death" or literally "death is no more." Eternally there will be no death in the New Jerusalem. Presently death is reigning in the physical world. The first human death did not come upon Adam or Cain, but it came upon the believing Abel. The first soul that left the earth went to heaven. The first man to meet death overcame it by God's grace. Death is a relief to a pained and infested body. Death is a release from decay and sin. However, only God is to determine the application of death (yes, He put capital punishment into the hand of the magistrate who must answer to Him)!

4) The destroyer of death. The Saviour by His death destroyed him that had the power of death, that is the devil (Heb. 2:14). The Saviour pursued death (John 4:34; Luke 12:50). One has said, "*Calvary*, with its *physical* phenomena—the trembling earth, the veiled sun, the darkened skies, the rent rocks, the opening greaves, the streaming blood, the bodily torture, the cry of woe; the *Cross*, with its more marvelous moral phenomena—the soul-sorrow, the mental darkness, the penitent thief, the shout of victory—all, all were vividly before Him every step He trod.... He never lost sight for a moment of Gethsemane or of Calvary."[19]

5) The deliverance from death. "There shall be no more death" (Rev. 21:4). "That as sin hath reigned unto death, even so might grace reign through righteousness unto eternal life by Jesus Christ our Lord" (Rom. 5:21). Believers in Christ are delivered from death. Christ abolished death—"Who hath abolished death, and hath brought life and immortality to light through the gospel" (2 Tim. 1:10). Christ repealed the law of death. Christ fulfilled the law to bring the repeal. He was made under the law, that He might redeem them that were under the law (Gal. 4:4). He abolished death by abolishing the law of death. He abolished death by His own actual and penal death. Thus saints only pass through the shadow of death. Death is a leaving of the body and going to be with the Lord, for the Christian. Christ abolished death in the Christians experience (Rom. 5:17). By bearing their sins Christ extracted the sting of death (1 Cor. 15:55-57). Robert E. Hough noted, "Speaking of the sting of death reminds one of the story which Dr. James M. Gray used to tell to

---

[19] Winslow, 154.

illustrate the removal of that sting. One summer day, a farmer was stung by a bee. Dr. Gray visited him at the time, and he told him about the incident. "Well," said the farmer, "there is one thing that brings me a good deal of satisfaction anyway; that bee will never sting another man!" "Why," asked his visitor, "did you kill it?" "No," he said, "but do you not know that a bee has only one sting, and when it stings a man, it leaves the sting in him?" Death has but one sting, and that one was lodged in the body of Christ on the cross (in behalf of all for whom He died). And since that is true, death may alight upon the believer, but there is no sting in it for him. Its power to torment is gone. Death is no longer the jailer of the grave, but the porter that opens the gate of paradise."[20] Christ delivers those who through fear of death were all their lifetime subject to bondage (Heb. 2:15). Death to the believer is the entrance to fullness of life because "blessed are the dead who die in the Lord."

6) The disappearance of death. "There shall be no more death" (Rev. 21:4). No more natural or spiritual death for the death of the body in this life is essential to the perfect freedom of the soul. The believer's death is a covenant of mercy. It is a release from his jail and it is an opening of the cage to allow him to soar to heaven. "Grace below is the dawn from glory above." The believer's resurrection body is free from the seeds of death. The present spiritual life will not pass through death for the Lord is in us here and we are in Him there. Saints already have everlasting life (John 3:36). We are more than conquerors (Rom. 8:34-35). We are never to perish (John 10:27-28). We shall be complete for He who began a good work of grace in us will perform it until the day of Jesus

[20] *The Christian After Death*, 16

244

Christ (Phil. 1:6). There will be no more spiritual deadness in our lives as now. There will be no coldness of heart or lack of love for Christ as now. Unbelief will be annihilated—fleshliness destroyed—selfishness eradicated—sin will not have a willing subject—and death will have no body to work on. The land where life is never lost, love is never chilled, zeal is never quenched, service is never tiring, songs are never ceasing, and the Lord is always present. The second death has no power over the citizens of the New Jerusalem (Rev. 20:5-6). Since believers are preparing to leave this world we need to tend to the purpose for our being in the world, God's glory in life and work. Jesus died and rose again that we may "not see death." Matthew Henry remarked, "Would you know where I am? I am at home in my Father's house, in the mansion prepared for me there. I am where I would be, where I have long and often desired to be—no longer on a stormy sea, but in a safe and quiet harbor. My working time is done, I am resting; my sowing time is done, I am reaping; my joy is at the time of harvest. Would you know how it is with me? I am made perfect in holiness; grace is swallowed up in glory; the top stone of the building is brought forth. Would you know what I AM DOING? I SEE God; I see him as He is, not as through a glass, darkly, but face to face; and the sight is transforming; it makes me like Him. I am in the sweet employment of my blessed Redeemer, my Head and Husband, whom my soul loved, and for whose sake I was willing to part with it all. I am here bathing myself at the spring-head of heavenly pleasures and joys unutterable; and, therefore weep not for me. I am here keeping a perpetual Sabbath; what that is, judge by your short Sabbaths. I am here singing hallelujahs incessantly to Him who sits upon the throne; and rest not day or night form praising him. Would you know what company I have? Blessed company, better than the best on earth—here are holy angels and the spirits of just men made perfect. I am set down with Abraham, and Isaac, and Jacob, in the kingdom of God, with blessed Paul and Peter, and James and John, and all the saints; and here I meet with many of my old acquaintance that I fasted and prayed with, who got before me hither. And lastly, would you consider how long this is to continue? It is a garland that never withers; a crown of glory that fades not away; after millions of millions of ages it will be as fresh as it is now; and, therefore, weep not for me."

7) The lessons from death. We learn of the brevity of life. We learn of the uncertainty of life. If fallen man lived forever on the earth some would worship money, some honor, some health, some beauty, some science, some man, etc. But since the brightest things are the flightiest there is a warning. Princes, scientists, governors, doctors, millionaires, etc. all die. The world passes away (1 John 2:17; Isa. 24:4 ff.). We learn that the arm of flesh will fail. We learn that preparation must be made for death and eternity (John 5:24). It is appointed unto men once to die and after that the judgment (Heb. 9:27). The hour of death is appointed by God in whose hand is the breath of life. Our duty is to be prepared to meet this unchangeable appointment. After the First Battle of Manassas Brig. Gen. John D. Imboden recorded his encounter with General T. J. "Stonewall" Jackson. "General Jackson's wound became very serious when inflammation set in. On hearing, three days after the fight, that he was suffering with it, I rode to his quarters, a little farm-house near Centreville. Although it was barely sunrise, he was out under the trees, bathing the hand with spring water. It was much swollen and very painful.... His wife had arrived the might before. Of course, the battle was the only topic discussed at breakfast. I remarked, in Mrs. Jackson's hearing, 'General, how is it that you can keep so cool, and appear so utterly insensible to danger in such a storm of shell and bullets as rained about you when your hand was hit?' He instantly became grave and reverential in his manner, and answered, in a low tone of great earnestness: 'Captain, my religious belief teaches me to feel as safe in battle as in bed. God has fixed the time of my death. I do not concern myself about that, but to be always ready, no matter when it may overtake me.' He added, after a pause, looking me full in the face: 'Captain, that is the way all men should live, and then all would be equally brave.' I felt that this last remark was intended as a rebuke for my profanity, when I had complained to him on the field.... He heard me, and simply said, 'Nothing can justify profanity.'"[21]

[6] John heard another promise from God— "And there shall be no more ... sorrow" (Rev. 21:4). Weeping caused by sorrow shall end and sorrow will be once and for all removed. The word for *"sorrow"* means a sorrow which cannot be concealed. Tears caused by sorrow shall be forever extinct in the New Jerusalem. There will be nothing to cause sorrow. However, in this life a Christian is not exempt from sorrow. He is possibly the most sensitive to it. When the question was asked, "What are these which are arrayed in white robes? and whence came they" (Rev. 7:13)? The answer was, "these are they which came out of great tribulation, and have washed their robes, and made

---

[21] *Battles and Leaders of the Civil War*, vol. 2, 238

them white in the blood of the Lamb" (Rev. 7:14). These came out of the school of suffering with degrees in sorrow.

Appendix 4

Christ's Pastoral Presence with His Dying People

John L. Girardeau

Minister & Professor of Theology in Columbia Theological Seminary

"Yea, though I walk through the valley of the shadow of death, I will fear no evil: for thou art with me; thy rod and thy staff they comfort me."—Psalm 23:4.

In this exquisite, sacred pastoral, the Psalmist of Israel celebrates, in touching strains, the constant and tender care which God exercises towards his covenant people. Under the beautiful imagery of a shepherd, leading his flock to green pastures and beside still waters, he is represented as conducting them to the rich provisions and the refreshing rest of the gospel. When, like wandering sheep, they deviate from his ways, he seeks them in love, collects them again with the pastoral crook, and guides them once more in the paths of righteousness and peace. When, in their waywardness and folly, they backslide from him, he still remembers his covenant, is faithful to his promises, and saves them for the sake of his own great name; and when they come to pass through the valley of the death-shade, his cheering presence dispels their fears, and his powerful grace proves their solace and support. Though it be true that Jehovah, the triune God, is the Shepherd of his people, there is a peculiar and emphatic sense in which Christ is represented in the gospel as sustaining the pastoral relation and discharging its functions. The Evangelist John reports him as declaring, "I am the Good Shepherd; the Good

Shepherd giveth his life for the sheep." The Apostle Paul speaks of the God of peace as having brought again from the dead our Lord Jesus, that Great Shepherd of the sheep, through the blood of the everlasting covenant. The Apostle Peter reminds believers that whereas they were in their natural condition as sheep going astray, they are now returned unto Christ as the Shepherd and Bishop of their souls. And the same apostle exhorts presbyters to feed the flock of God in view of the reward which the Great Pastor would eventually confer upon them: "And when the Chief Shepherd shall appear, ye shall receive a crown of glory that fadeth not away." These passages make it sufficiently evident that the Lord Jesus is peculiarly the Shepherd of his people.

The pastoral relation is a comprehensive one, including the three offices which Christ, as Mediator, sustains: those of a Prophet, a Priest and a King. As it is the province of a shepherd to feed his flock, to rule and protect them from their enemies, and, if necessary, to lay down his life in their defense, the prophetical function, by which Jesus feeds his people, the kingly, by which he rules and protects them, and the sacerdotal, by which he redeems them through his death, are all embraced in his pastoral office. It touches the interests, the experience and the hopes of believers at every point, both in life and in death. It involves the application of a Saviour's power, love and mercy to their every emergency and their every need. With infinite tenderness compassion and vigilance, the great Pastor follows his sheep through every devious path of life, and extends to them his succor when they faint under burning suns, in the horrid wilderness, and amidst the glooms and terrors of the shadow of death.

I. In the first place, it may be remarked in attempting to expand the comforting truths suggested by the text, that the pastoral presence of Jesus is a protection to the dying believer from the fears of evil which would otherwise distress him. "When I walk through the valley of the shadow of death I will fear no evil, for thou art with me." I have no objection to render to the view which makes these words applicable to those critical passages in the life of God's people, which may not inappropriately be described as the valley of the death-shade. This was evidently the interpretation of that masterly delineator of Christian experience, John Bunyan, in his immortal allegory. He represents his pilgrim as struggling with the dangers and conflicts of the valley of the shadow of death before he comes to the crossing of the last river. And it cannot be disputed that there are seasons in the experience of the believer, when, pressed by his besetting temptations, pursued by the malice of the devil, and fascinated by the enchantments or persecuted by the fury of the world, he encounters terrors which are akin to those of death itself. In these fearful exigencies, these periods of conflict, depression and anguish, he appears to be passing down into the darkness and gloom of the valley of death; and it is the pastoral presence of Christ in the hour of despair which dissipates the fear of evil and lights up the soul with returning joy and peace. But although this be true, I see no reason for disturbing the ordinary interpretation placed upon the words of the text—an interpretation which makes them specially applicable to the passage of the believer through death, and one which has proved a charm to dispel the apprehensions of ill from the bosoms of thousands of

Christ's people amidst the doubts, the strifes, the agonies of the dying hour.

There are three great and notable epochs in the earthly history of the believer in Jesus. The first is that in which, at the creative fiat of the Almighty Maker, he springs from nonentity into being, and is confronted with the duties, the responsibilities and the bliss or woe of an immortal career. The next is that in which, by virtue of a second creation and through the wondrous process of the new birth and conversion, he passes from the kingdom of Satan and of darkness into the kingdom of grace and of light. From being a bondsman of the devil, a slave of sin and an heir of hell, he becomes, by a marvelous transformation, a subject of God, a citizen of heaven, and an inheritor of everlasting possessions and an amaranthine crown. It is a transitional process which awakens the pulse of a new life, engenders the habits of holiness, adorns the soul with the rich graces of the divine Spirit, and inspires the joyful hope of eternal felicity beyond the grave. The third, and it is the most solemn and terrible crisis of his being, is that of death, in which the believer passes through nature's closing conflict and the awful change of dissolution to the experience of an untried existence. The transition is suited to alarm. It is nothing less than one from time to eternity, and it is accomplished in the twinkling of an eye. At one moment he is surrounded by the familiar objects of earth, and looks upon the faces of his weeping friends who cluster around the bed of death, and in the next he opens his eyes upon eternal realities and the blaze of God's immediate presence. Nature, (was) constructed originally for an immortal life, instinctively recoils from so violent and revolting a change as that which death involves. It shrinks back in terror from the vision of the coffin and the shroud, of the corruption and the worms of the grave. The circumstances attending the dying process are such as are suited to appall a conscious sinner, and fill him with consternation and dismay—the cruel rupture of earthly relations, the sudden withdrawal of accustomed scenes, the forced abandonment of wonted pursuits, the absolute loneliness of the passage, the dread neighborhood of the flaming bar and the rigor of the last account. My brethren, how shall we, without apprehension, encounter so tremendous a change? The text furnishes us an answer which illumines the gloom of the dying chamber, and lights up the darkness of the grave. The pastoral presence of the Lord Jesus is an antidote to the fears, and a preventive of the evils, of death. There are two modes by which this blessed result is accomplished:

i. In the first place the Great Shepherd accompanies the believer in his last passage as the Conqueror of Death. That which chiefly renders death an object of terror is the consciousness of guilt. The groans, the pains, the dissolution of our bodily organisms, are confessedly dreadful and repulsive; but the great poet was right when he intimated that it is conscience, a guilty conscience forecasting the retributions of the future, which makes cowards of us all. It is this which leads us to shrink from the dying bed as an arena of battle, and from the last struggle as a hopeless conflict with an evil which the startled imagination personates as a monarch and invests with power to destroy. Death becomes the king of terrors. Were there no sin, the change which might have been necessary to remove us from the present state and to adapt us to another would have been an easy and delightful translation, a euthanasia, disquieted by no apprehensions of the soul,

253

and disturbed by no pains of the body. But sin has clothed death with its tyrannical prerogative as a universal and remorseless despot, converted the world into a melancholy theatre of his triumphs, and transformed the earth into a vast graveyard, whitened with the monuments of his sway. The removal from the present state becomes a passage through a valley of tears peopled with shapes of terror, and encompassed with the darkness of the death-shade.

Christ has subdued this dreadful monster. He conquered death by conquering sin, and he overcomes sin by his dying obedience to law. This is the statement of the apostle in his argument touching the resurrection of the body: "The sting of death is sin." The power of death to inflict torture, to poison our happiness and blast our hopes, lies in the fact that we are guilty, and are, therefore, completely subjected to his tyranny. "The strength of sin is the law." The punishment of our guilt is penal. Our dying sufferings are the penalty of a broken law; and sin, in inflicting them upon us, throws itself back for the enforcement of its authority upon the irreversible sanctions of that majestic and eternal rule which we have outraged and insulted. Christ has stripped sin of this strength. He has unnerved the cruel monarch, and rendered him powerless to destroy his people. The glorious Redeemer, moved by compassion for our wretched estate, came down to our relief and stood forth as the champion of his church in her conflict with death. He assumed our guilt, took the sting of death in his own soul, underwent our penal sufferings and, in accordance with the law of substitution, relieved us from the obligation to suffer the same punishment, and has enlisted the divine justice on the side of our deliverance. Christ has died penally for his people. God accepts the vicarious sacrifice, and the believer cannot die in the same way. Justice cannot demand a double payment of the same debt. Death is divested of its penal feature, and is transformed from a curse into a blessing, from a passage to execution into a translation to bliss. In the tragedy enacted on the cross, Jesus, the representative of his people, engaged in a mighty wrestle with Death. He fell, but his fall crushed out the life of his dread antagonist. He died, but death died with him. He was buried, but he dragged death down with him into the grave; and there, despoiling the tyrant of his diadem, he unfurled over his crownless head the ensign of his people's salvation, and, in their name, took undisputed possession of his whole domain. It is true that the believer must still pass through the dying change, but the curse of it is forever gone. It is no more death in its true and awful sense as the penalty of law. "I," says the divine Redeemer, "I am the resurrection and the life; he that believeth in me, though he were dead, yet shall he live; and he that liveth and believeth in me shall never die." "He that keepeth my sayings shall never see death." It is true that the believer must die; but in dying he is privileged to suffer with his Master, that he may rise and reign with him. It is true that the believer must die; but death now constitutes part of a wholesome discipline which prepares him for glory; it is a process by which he is purged from dross, casts off the slough of corruption, and is purified for his admission into the holy presence of God and the sanctified communion of saints. It is true that he must walk through the dark valley; but the Conqueror of Death descends into it by his side, illuminates its darkness by the radiance of his presence, protects him from the assaults of a now powerless foe, and bearing in his hands the keys of death and the invisible world, peacefully dismisses the departing saint from sin to holiness, and from the stormy trials of earth to the joy and peace of an everlasting rest.

ii. It may be observed further, that the pastoral presence of Jesus with his dying people is manifested by the tender ministration of his sympathy. There were two great ends which the Saviour contemplated in his sufferings and death—the one that he might redeem his people from sin and everlasting punishment; the other that he might be qualified by experience to sympathize with them while themselves passing through the afflictions of life and the pains of the dying hour. To achieve these results, he became incarnate, partook of our nature, and was made bone of our bone and flesh of our flesh. Not merely a legal substitute, but possessed of the sublime and tender spirit of a priest, he consented to be compassed with sinless infirmity that he might be capable of compassion for the weak, the wandering and the dying. An infirm human being, struggling under the burden of assumed guilt, and confronted by the terrors of divine wrath, is it any marvel that he looked forward to death not without fear? One of the most affecting and pathetic passages in the Scriptures is that in which the apostle, discoursing of the priestly sufferings of Jesus, tells us that in the days of his flesh he offered up prayers and supplications with strong crying and tears unto him that was able to save him from death, and was heard in that he feared. For it must be remembered, that the form of death which Christ encountered, while it included the experience of our sufferings, embraced incomparably more. In his own person, perfectly innocent, and in his character stainlessly holy, he merited intrinsically the admiration of his fellow-men, and the approval of his

God. So far from deserving to die, he was entitled, on the naked score of retributive justice, to the highest and most blissful life. And yet condescending, in boundless mercy, to be treated as putatively (or reputedly to be) guilty for the sake of dying men, he underwent a form of death, the least element of which was the pains of dissolution—a death which involved the experience of infinite wrath and the intolerable pains of hell. The cup which was placed in the hands of Jesus in Gethsemane was one which was never offered to any other human being on earth. The trembling and consternation of his human nature as he took that chalice of woe, his thrice-repeated prayer to be relieved, if possible, from the necessity of drinking it, and the bloody sweat that swathed his body like a robe, attested an anguish of soul which none but he was ever called upon to bear. The Sufferer, who, for us, expired on the cross of Calvary, endured a species of death which was as singular as it was comprehensive and exhaustive. In body, he suffered the keen and protracted tortures of crucifixion; and in spirit, reviled by foes, deserted by friends and abandoned of God, he descended alone into the valley of the death-shade, which was not only veiled in impenetrable gloom, but swept by the tempests of avenging wrath. Furnished with such an experience, the Good Shepherd ministers with exquisite sympathy at the couch of the dying believer. He knows his doubts, his apprehensions, his fears; and, moved by a compassion which naught but a common suffering could produce, he makes all the bed under the expiring saint, smooths his last pillow, and "wipes his latest tear away."

II. In the second place, the Psalmist beautifully portrays the consoling influence of Christ's presence upon the dying believer when he represents the pastoral staff as affording him protection and comfort. "Thy rod and thy staff, they comfort me." The staff, the appropriate emblem of the pastoral office, may be regarded in two aspects. As a rod, it is a powerful weapon of defense; and as a staff, it is an instrument of support. It is at once, therefore, the symbol of protecting power and of supporting grace. When at eventide the oriental shepherd had folded his flock, and missed from the number some crippled ewe or tender lamb, he failed not, albeit through night and storm, to go in quest of the wanderer as it strayed amid the jagged rocks of the mountain-side, or the terrors of the howling wilderness. And when he had found it, he gathered it compassionately in his arms, laid it upon his shoulders, and took his way homeward rejoicing. But often he was compelled to pass through some deep and gloomy gorge, infested by wild beasts and rendered dangerous by the swollen torrent dashing fiercely through it and making the passage hazardous and the foothold insecure. Then, when from some neighboring thicket the young lion sprang forth and roared upon his prey, wielding his shepherd's staff as a weapon of defense, he protected the precious burden he carried, and beat back the assailant to his lair; or, as he stepped from one slippery rock to another, through the rapid current, he used his staff as a supporting prop, and stayed both himself and the feeble wanderer which he conducted to the folded flock. Thus it is, my brethren, with the Great Shepherd and Bishop of souls, when, in the night of death, he leads the feeble and dying members of his flock through the valley of the death-shade to the heavenly fold. There are two difficulties which the believer has not unfrequently to encounter when he comes to die:

In the first place, he is liable to the last and desperate assaults of the adversary of souls. Baffled by the power of the everlasting covenant in his attempts to compass the destruction of the believer, he meets him at the bed of death, and taking advantage of his helplessness, endeavors, if he cannot destroy him, to mar the peace and becloud the prospect of his latest moments on earth. He showers his fiery darts upon him, injects doubts as to his acceptance with God, conjures up from the past the apparition of his sins, and calls up before his appalled imagination the vision of an angry Judge, a fiery bar, and a night of eternal despair. But another and a greater than Satan is there. The Chief Shepherd is also in that chamber of death. Standing at the dying bedside, and lifting his pastoral staff as a rod of defense, he wards off from his agonized servant the incursions of the powers of darkness, and beats back the assaults of his Satanic foes.

Another difficulty which is apt to disturb the peace of the departing believer is derived from his vivid remembrance of his sins, and his consequent fear that he is not prepared to meet his God. In the solemn and honest hour of death, his soul, conscious of its dread proximity to the judgment seat, takes a minute and impartial survey of the past. His memory, quickened into an energy which only death can impart, with lightning rapidity sweeps, as at a glance, the whole field of his earthly history. There is no glazing process then by which the hideous features of his sins can be painted or concealed, no apology for his crimes which will stand the scrutiny of the death-bed, or abide the breaking light of the eternal world. All his acts of youthful folly, all his broken vows, all his unredeemed promises to his God, all his fearful backslidings, all his sinful thoughts, words and deeds, now crowd into his dying chamber, throng around his dying bed, and threaten to go with him as swift witnesses against him before the final bar. The billows of a fiercer death than that of the body dash over his head, and, struggling in the torrent which threatens to sweep him through the last valley downward to a bottomless abyss; he cries in his extremity to the Redeemer of his soul. Never deaf to the appeals of his dying people, the Great Shepherd hastens to his relief with the succors of his supporting grace. He whispers to the sinking believer that he died to save him, that his blood has cleansed him of all his sins, and that his perfect righteousness, his atoning merit, is a ground of acceptance, a foundation that will not fail him when the wicked and unbelieving shall be driven from the divine presence like the chaff before the storm. It is enough. The dying believer, with the hand of faith, grasps the pastoral staff that Jesus thus extends to him, and, leaning upon it, passes in safety through the glooms and dangers of the death-shade, emerges into the light of heaven, and is satisfied with the beatific vision of God.

Fellow-travelers to the dark valley, let us believe in Jesus as our Saviour. Let us put our trust m him as the Shepherd and Bishop of our souls. So when we are called to die, no guilty conscience will break our peace, no condemning law will thunder upon us, no frowns of an angry Judge will deepen the awful shadow of death; but we will fear no evil, for Christ will be with us; his rod will protect us in our last conflict, his staff will support us in our latest pang.

Bibliography

SETS

Boice, James Montgomery. *An Expositional Commentary on Psalms*, 3 Volumes. Grand Rapids: Baker Books, 2000.

Carroll, B. H. *An Interpretation of the English Bible*, 17 Volumes. Grand Rapids: Baker Book House, 1976.

Clarke, Adam. *The Holy Bible: Commentary and Critical Notes*, 6 Volumes, London: William Tegg, n.d.

Cook, F. C. (Editor). *The Bible Commentary*. Grand Rapids: Baker Book House, (1879).

Dickson, David. *A Commentary on the Psalms*, 2 Volumes. London: the Banner of Truth Trust, (1653-5) 1965.

Ellicott, Charles John. *An Old Testament Commentary for English Readers*, 5 Volumes . London: Cassell and Company, Limited, 1897.

Gill, John. *A Complete Body of Doctrinal and Practical Divinity: A System of Evangelical Truths*, 2 Volumes. London: Thomas Tegg, 1839.

Gill, John. *An Exposition of the Old Testament*, 4 Volumes. London: William Hill Collingridge, 1853.

Hall, Joseph, *The Works of*, 12 Volumes, Oxford: D. A. Talboys, 1837.

Henry, Matthew. *An Exposition of the Historical Books of the Old Testament*, 3 Volumes. London: J. Clarke, E. Matthews, et. al., 1721.

Jamieson, Robert. *A Commentary Critical, Experimental and Practical*, 6 Volumes. Grand Rapids: Wm. B. Eerdmans Publishing Co., 1945.

Keil, C. F. and Delitzsch, F. *Biblical Commentary on the Old Testament,* 25 Volumes. Grand Rapids: Wm. B. Eerdmans Publishing Company, 1963.

Hengstenberg, E. W. *Commentary on the Psalms*, 3 Volumes. Cherry Hill: Mack Publishing Company, n.d.

Kitto, John. *Daily Bible Illustration,* 7 Volumes. Edinburgh: William Oliphant and Co., 1867.

Kitto, John. *The Illustrated Family Bible*, 2 Volumes. London: James Sangster and Company, n.d.

Mason, John M. *The Writings of*, 4 Volumes. New York: Ebenezer Mason, 1832.

Nicoll, W. R., Editor. *The Expositor's Bible*, 49 Volumes. New York: A. C. Armstrong and Son, 1896.

Patrick, Lowth, Arnald, Whitby, and Lowman. *A Critical Commentary and Paraphrase on the Old and New Testament*, 4 Volumes. London: William Tegg and Co., 1849.

Perowne, J. J. Stewart. *The Book of Psalms: A New Translation with Introductions and Notes*, 2 Volumes. Andover: Warren F. Draper, 1879.

Plumptre, E. H. Editor, *The Bible Educator*, 4 Volumes. London: Cassell, Petter, Galpin & Co. n.d.

Poole, Matthew. *Annotations upon the Holy Bible*, 3 Volumes. London: James Nisbet and Co., 1855.

Scroggie, W. Graham. *The Psalms*, 4 Volumes. London: Pickering & Inglis LTD., 1948.

Spence, H. D. M. & Exell, Joseph S. Editors, *The Pulpit Commentary*, 23 Volumes. Grand Rapids: Wm. B. Eerdmans Publishing Company, 1962.

Spurgeon, C. H. *The Treasury of David*, 8 Volumes. London: Passmore and Alabaster, 1870

Trapp, John. *A Commentary on the Old and New Testaments*, 6 Volumes. Eureka: Tanski Publications, 1997.

Wiener, Philip P., Editor. *Dictionary of the History of Ideas: Studies of Selected Pivotal Ideas*, 5 Volumes. New York: Charles Scribner's Sons, 1973.

Wines, E. C. *Commentaries on the Laws of the Ancient Hebrews*. New York: Geo. P. Putnam & Co., 1855.

INDIVIDUAL VOLUMES

Alexander, Joseph Addison. *The Psalms Translated and Explained*. Grand Rapids: Baker Book House, (1873) 1975.

Alexander, William. *The Witness of the Psalms to Christ and Christianity*. London: John Murray, 1890.

Allen, Charles L. *Victory in the Valleys of Life*. Minneapolis: Grason, 1981.

Baker, Sir. Richard. *Meditations and Disquisitions upon the First Psalm; The Penitential Psalms; and Seven Consolatory Psalms*. Harrisonburg: Sprinkle Publications, (1639-1640) 1988.

Binnie, William. *A Pathway into the Psalter*. Birmingham: Solid Ground Christian Books, (1886) 2005.

Bonar, Andrew A. *Christ and His Church in the Book of Psalms*. New York: Robert Carter & Brothers, 1860.

Campbell, Murdoch. *From Grace to Glory: Meditations on the Book of Psalms*. London: The Banner of Truth Trust, 1970.

Dallimore, Arnold. *The Life of Edward Irving: Fore-runner of the Charismatic Movement*. Edinburgh: The Banner of Truth Trust, 1983.

Davis, John J. *The Perfect Shepherd: Studies in the Twenty-third Psalm*. Grand Rapids: Baker Book House, 1980.

Davis, Noah K. *Juda's Jewels: A Study in the Hebrew Lyrics*. Nashville: Methodist Episcopal Church, South, 1896.

Evans, William. *The Shepherd Psalm and Looking Beyond*. Chicago: Moody Press, 1932.

Griffith, Leonard. *God in Man's Experience*. Waco: Word Books, 1968.

Horne, George. *A Commentary on the Book of Psalms*. New York: Robert Carter, 1845.

Keller, Phillip. *A Shepherd Looks at Psalm 23*. Grand Rapids: Zondervan, 1975.

Ketcham, R. T. *"I Shall Not Want:" An Exposition of Psalm Twenty-three*. Chicago: Moody Press, 1967.

Killen, J. M. *Our Friends in Heaven: The Mutual Recognition of the Redeemed in Glory Demonstrated*. Philadelphia: Presbyterian Board of Publication, nd.

Leupold, H. C. *Exposition of the Psalms*. Grand Rapids: Baker Book House, (1959) 1972.

MacMillan, J. Douglas. *The Lord Our Shepherd*. Bridgend: Evangelical Press of Wales, 1986.

Maclaren, Alexander. *The Life of David as Reflected in His Psalms*. Edinburgh: MacNiven & Wallace, 1880.

McCullagh, Archibald. *Beyond the Stars; or Human Life in Heaven*. New York: Anson D. F. Randolph & Company, 1889.

Meyer, F. B. *F. B. Meyer on the Psalms: Bible Readings*. Grand Rapids: Zondervan Publishing House, n.d.

Meyer, F. B. *The Shepherd Psalm*. New York: Fleming H. Revell Company, 1889.

Murphy, James G. *A Critical and Exegetical Commentary on the Book of Psalms, with a New Translation*. Minneapolis: James Family Publishing, (1876) 1977.

Ogilvie, Lloyd John. *Falling into Greatness*. Carmel: Guideposts, 1984.

Plumer, William S. *Psalms: A Critical and Expository Commentary with Doctrinal and Practical Remarks*. Edinburgh: The Banner of Truth Trust, (1867) 1975.

Rumburg, H. Rondel. *The Universal Dominion of Christ: A Study in Psalm 2*. Birmingham: Society for Biblical and Southern Studies, 1996.

Sedgwick, Obadiah. *The Shepherd of Israel or God's Pastoral Care Over His People*. London: D. Maxwell, 1658.

Slemming, C. W. *He Leadeth Me: Shepherd Life in Palestine*. Fort Washington: Christian Literature Crusade, 1964.

Stedman, Ray C. *Folk Psalms of Faith*. Glendale: G / L Publications, 1973.

Stevenson, John. *The Lord Our Shepherd: An Exposition of the Twenty-Third Psalm*, New York: Reformed Protestant Dutch Church, 1859.

Tucker, Henry H. *The Gospel in Enoch or Truth in the Concrete*. Appomattox: SBSS, 2016 (1868).

Winslow, Octavius. *Help Heavenward: or Words of Strength and Heart-Cheer to Zion's Travellers*. London: James Nisbet & Co., 1882.

Winslow, Octavius. *Pisgah Views: or The Negative Aspects of Heaven*. London: John F. Shaw & Co., 1873.

Yates, Kyle M. *Preaching from the Psalms*. New York: Harper & Brothers Publishers, 1948.

Yates, Kyle M. *Studies in Psalms*. Nashville: Broadman Press, 1953.

267

270

271